The Genius
of Jewish Celebrities

"Dr. Robby" holds a doctorate degree in Psychology and is president of Ramya International, a company that specializes in applying graphology (expert handwriting analysis) and pertinent psychology methods. He has helped corporations place the right executives into the right positions and win contracts. Dr. Yaronne is also an expert in jury selection, utilizing graphology to predict the thinking and decision-making style of potential jurors.

Dr. Robby has been teaching clinical psychology since 1979 in various colleges and universities throughout the world. He has been a guest-expert on NBC and ABC, analyzing the handwriting of celebrities, criminals, and others. When NBC handed him 20 handwriting samples, without any background information, he was able to distinguish, with perfect accuracy, between nuns and convicted criminals for the TV program "Honesty, Dishonesty in America."

I dedicate this book to my late mother, Ina Yaronne-Lucas, who encouraged me throughout my life to be a keen researcher of the mind.

I thank Gadi Inbar, whose wonderful guidance helped to add zest to the book's appearance, and those who were in charge of the resulting artwork: Carolyn McEwen and Tom Bugzavich. I also want to acknowledge Yoram Kahana from Shooting Star and Tsipi Sover from Tel Aviv's Beit Ariela Library for their help with the photographic material. Many thanks to Frances Agliata, Eli Kedem, Ron Podchlebnik, and Jack Zemer for helping to make this book a reality. I thank my fiancée whose editorial and production inputs were priceless. Last but not least, my gratitude goes to the Supreme Being who made it all possible and brought such accomplished and helpful people into my life.

The Genius of Jewish Celebrities

What their handwriting reveals

DR. ROBERT YARONNE

HIGH PUBLISHING • SAN DIEGO

table of contents

Copyright ©2009 High Publishing

All rights reserved.
Registered with the Library of Congress.

No part of the contents of this book may be reproduced without the written consent of the publisher.

High Publishing
PO Box 4653
Carmel Mt. Rd.
Suite 308 #120
San Diego, CA 92130

Printed in Israel by Meiri Press

ISBN: 978-0-9769452-0-8

Biographies, Jewish, Graphology, Psychology, History

what is GRAPHOLOGY?

What is Handwriting Analysis?

Handwriting analysis or Graphology is the science of personality profiling based on the way people write. A skilled graphologist can detect major personality trends from a simple signature.

Advantages of Handwriting Analysis

The advantage of Graphology in comparison to other psychological tests is that the graphologist doesn't have to meet face to face with the person they are analyzing, nor do they have to administer hours of psychological testing. This very important facet enables us to bring you, in this book, personality sketches and secrets of Jewish celebrities without the need to interview them in person. Whether deceased or currently at the pinnacle of their success in their particular area of expertise, it's just a handwriting sample that brings us inside the minds of these great movers and shakers. Graphology is the accurate, objective science that tells us how things really are without the intervention of public relations agents; the secrets that their handwriting could not hide.

Graphology and Secrets

When a person writes, he or she discloses his or her past, personality, and attitudes about all sorts of things. The writer is not aware of this fact because writing is a very automatic process in modern society. We all possess secrets, strengths and weaknesses, which curve their influence into our subconscious which essentially controls our behavior, revealed in our handwriting. In a quick and careful glimpse, a graphologist will be able to tell how creative, insane, generous, sensual, entrepreneurial, destructive or genius you are.

What can handwriting teach us?

Handwriting covers five major areas of life:

1. **The subject's intelligence level and how their mind and thought processes work.**

   Is the writer analytical or intuitive? How high is his/her I.Q.? How accurate and pedantic can he/she be? How creative and original is the writer? What compulsions do they have? What style of thinking does the writer employ?

   For example:
   the small analytical handwriting of **Jonas Salk,**

   versus the flamboyant handwriting of **Bette Midler.**

2. **Self esteem, self concept**

   How the person perceives oneself is very important. It is said that Hitler and Napoleon compensated for their perceived inferiority complex by conquering Europe. How a person perceives the self, determines much of their behavior and attitude.

An objective science that reveals the twists and turns of the human psyche through the precise and careful analysis of handwriting.

3. Emotions

We always want to know about a person's emotional sphere. Are they temperamental, warm or cold? Are they capable of expressing their emotions? How does the celebrity control his/her emotions? Are they grouchy, hot tempered, demonstrative, or inward bound?

For example:
Are they warm in nature like **Jerry Seinfeld**,

or grouchy and critical like **Albert Einstein?**

4. Anxiety and defenses

Every celebrity has a secret anxiety. Whether it is the fear of flying, one's fear of success, fear of gender identity, or of a general nature. Handwriting analysis can show how the Jewish celebrity is dealing with their anxiety. Anxiety can explain many of the moves and behaviors of the celebrities, which are portrayed through the media.

For example: **Barbara Streisand's** social anxiety is shown through her signature.

5. Social relations

Here we want to know how the celebrity handles interpersonal relations. What is the truth behind the social mask also know as persona? How is their sex life? What style do they possess when interacting with other people? Are they outgoing, extroverted with leadership abilities, or more introverted, withdrawn and shy? How honest is the celebrity? Would you let him/her keep your last $50?

For example:
Are they diplomatic and sly like **Henry Kissinger**,

or bold and open like **Larry King?**

Through this book, we shall shed light on particular graphological signs, so you, the reader, can learn the secrets of how to become your own graphologist.

introduction

The Jewish people are some of the most fascinating and persevering in the world. Despite millennia of persecution, a holocaust and centuries of near-genocides, deportation and wars, they've somehow managed to survive, keeping their faith and traditions alive and in tact.

Some say their secret lies in the understanding they share with the Almighty, and the Almighty's commitment to the Jews as "the chosen people." Jews from all around the world take pride in their heritage and having overcome lifetimes of hardship and mass migrations while maintaining a sense of love and community all along the way. They are considered by many an exceptionally gifted people and nation. Although their share of the population of the United States is less than one percent, 61 percent of the Nobel Prize winners in Economics are Jewish. Every major breakthrough in civilization has involved someone from the Jewish race: Broadway, Hollywood, the Polio vaccine, psychoanalysis, the Atom Bomb and so much more. You could even refer to monotheism as originally being a Jewish belief that transformed religions to come, a major contribution to the world.

This book will address and achieve three major issues:

1. First and foremost, it not only acknowledges Jewish celebrities, but also sheds light on their innermost motives and secrets. We do this by looking at their handwriting through the science of graphology.

2. Address and hope to bring to an end, countless years of negative propaganda and stereotypes that have spurred anti-Semitism throughout the world.

3. Help to fire-up the dignity of the Jewish people by showing their humanity and accomplishments.

Each of the featured celebrities will be revealed in four ways –

1. The "call out" – a "punch line" distilling the essence of the celebrity's personality.

2. A short biography – excellent for schools and scholars to study.

3. Four revealing facts – drawn from the overall assessment of the handwriting and....

4. Six to nine secrets drawn from the particular indicators of the handwriting. You don't have to be an expert to enjoy this section.

This book is divided into nine sections: entertainers, scientists, sports, musicians and artists, philosophers, entrepreneurs, writers, politicians and Israelis. The goal is to entertain and enrich your understanding and appreciation of the Jewish geniuses and the secrets that can be deciphered through understanding each detail of personal handwriting through graphology.

entertainers

larry KING

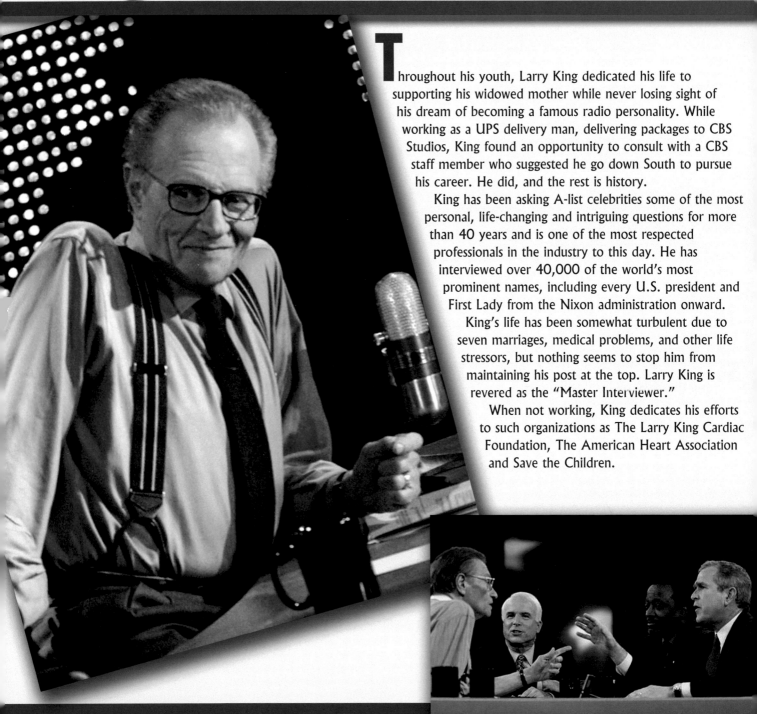

Throughout his youth, Larry King dedicated his life to supporting his widowed mother while never losing sight of his dream of becoming a famous radio personality. While working as a UPS delivery man, delivering packages to CBS Studios, King found an opportunity to consult with a CBS staff member who suggested he go down South to pursue his career. He did, and the rest is history.

King has been asking A-list celebrities some of the most personal, life-changing and intriguing questions for more than 40 years and is one of the most respected professionals in the industry to this day. He has interviewed over 40,000 of the world's most prominent names, including every U.S. president and First Lady from the Nixon administration onward.

King's life has been somewhat turbulent due to seven marriages, medical problems, and other life stressors, but nothing seems to stop him from maintaining his post at the top. Larry King is revered as the "Master Interviewer."

When not working, King dedicates his efforts to such organizations as The Larry King Cardiac Foundation, The American Heart Association and Save the Children.

the handwriting reveals:

- Articulate and visionary, imaginative, and philosophically and spiritually open-minded.

- Good mixture of an analytical sharp mind, generosity and patience.

- King is creative, independent and tolerant. He sees possibilities in any situation and can deal creatively with changes.

- Slow to become irritated or upset.

He has interviewed over 40,000 of the world's most prominent names, including every U.S. president and First Lady from the Nixon administration onward.

1. Capital **"L"** is not connected to the name: indicates the writer takes time to think before shooting from the hip.

2. The hook-hold on the **"L"** indicates the writer enjoys compliments and praise. Also, the writer seeks gratification from food.

3. The upper zone of **"L"** is a full loop: expansiveness, generosity. He is likely to give to charity.

4. The **"K"** love knot: a liking for people and sex.

5. The **"a"** angles: analytical, likes challenges. The writer is professional with a conscience, has great self-discipline and can be a very thorough negotiator. He does not dodge responsibilities. He can display highly intelligent and philosophic thinking. He must be active.

6. The **"K"** end stroke, short of the base line: reveals a very ambitious personality.

7. The tooth-like **"r"** suggests he is able to get to the bottom of hard issues.

8. The **"g"** shows he can tolerate routine or rote tasks.

9. Very sensitive imagination.

11

Jerry has a collection of over 500 sneakers.
They are all white.

1. The capital **"J"** full lower zone loop indicates sexual imagination and love of money.

2. The **"r"** shows dexterity and versatility.

3. The capital **"S"** is simple and like an open number 8: The writer is constantly on the lookout for new ideas.

4. The **"i"** dot is a dash indicating a lot of animation and vibrancy.

5. The **"i"** dot is high to the right: The writer has aspirations to surpass his present position and focus on long-range goals. He is very enthusiastic, uninhibited and able to set high standards. He can relate to the whole rather than the parts.

6. The **"l"** loop is tall and full, indicating a person with a great deal of idealism.

7. The **"d"** loop is tall and full, suggesting that the writer is very sensitive and at times becomes overly emotional. It can also mean he always trusts people fully.

8. The **"n"** has two peaks: The writer is very analytical.

9. The **"y"** lower loop is full and long, suggesting a very sexual personality.

jerry SEINFELD

Jerry Seinfeld grew up on Long Island, under the influence of a father with a terrific sense of humor. He went straight from college to amateur night try-out at New York's "Catch a Rising Star," and was soon seen all over the state of New York performing in local clubs and at Catskill Mountain resorts. A Rodney Dangerfield HBO special in 1976 gave his career a huge boost, and when he was abruptly cut from the "Benson" (1979) sitcom, he swore he'd never participate in another television show that diminished his creative control.

In 1980 Seinfeld moved to Los Angeles where he made his first appearance on the "Tonight Show" and America instantly fell in love with him. He also became a favorite, reoccurring guest on "Late Night with David Letterman" as well as various HBO Specials. By the late 1980s he was one of the busiest comedians in the country, making about 300 appearances each year. His signature accomplishment, "The Jerry Seinfeld Show," garnered huge ratings, lasted 8 years, and put him "on the map" forever.

He is known for his impeccable neatness, a compulsive habit of throwing out the clothes he travels with after each road trip, and his collection of over 500 sneakers – all white.

the handwriting reveals:

- His writing shows a tendency toward the neurotic, which actually engenders his creativity.

- May have a strong materialistic and sensual side with a lot of built-up frustration.

- Tendency towards moodiness.

- May have some emotional ambivalence regarding his parents, and, at times he may feel that he carries too many responsibilities.

goldie HAWN

Master comedienne Goldie Hawn began her performance career as a ballet dancer. Her mother ran a dance school and Goldie began teaching there as a teenager, running her own ballet classes throughout her college years. Two years later she moved to New York City to pursue acting and dance professionally, and as fate would have it, ended up on "Laugh-In" (1968-1970) as a go-go dancer, which earned her an Emmy! The show's success and the stress that came with it helped to induce a nervous breakdown from which she recovered. Nothing stopped Hawn from reaching her ultimate success as she went on to act and star in over 30 films, many nominated for top awards around the globe. She's now one of Hollywood's most durable, powerful, and respected celebrities.

Hawn has been married several times. She credits her marriage break-ups to men who couldn't handle her fame, and refers to herself a "light personality with a deep-thinking brain."

the handwriting reveals:

- Playful, young at heart, and not afraid to express herself.

- Effervescent and bubbly personality.

- She may be worried about her appearance and the effect of her looks on her popularity.

- Tendency to react strongly to emotional stress.

Nothing stopped Hawn from reaching her ultimate success as she went on to act and star in over 30 films, many nominated for top awards around the globe.

1. The signature is too illegible, which means she feels the need to hide her true identity. She likes to be different and appear mysterious; there is some kind of selfishness indicated here.

3. The last stroke goes down and under the baseline: At times this writer can be hurtful to oneself, but doesn't want to hurt other people.

2. The high arc over the **"G"** means a subconscious need to protect oneself.

the SIGNATURE

On Friday afternoon I will be going to Seattle
Sonia Schmuland

If the signature is an extension of the script and similar to the rest of the text, the writer is not hiding behind a name badge. He is, in his signature, what he appears to be in his writing. This points to an unaffected person; someone who does not put on airs.

ON FRIDAY MORNING I WILL BE GOING TO JAY'S LUGGAE.

On the other hand, significant differences between text and signature indicate a discrepancy between form and content; the desired impression versus the writer's real nature. There are writers who wish to present themselves in a certain way. The psychological reasons for embellishing can come from lack of self-esteem and the need to compensate for subjective inadequacies.

Have a good day

If the signature is larger than the writing, the writer is posing. This can mean a desire to impress or to create a shield against outside influences. In fact, the writer is actually more modest than he or she appears to be.

Ida and I are going to Italy.

A signature that is smaller than the writing shows a writer who may be less modest than otherwise thought to be. In this case the truth is contrary to appearances. This is a classic case of Freud's "reaction formation," a defense mechanism whereby the person changes his true nature in order to avoid anxiety from exposing his true feelings.

All the Best!
Mel Brooks

The slant in the signature has significance, it indicates social attitude. If a signature slants to the right the writer is outgoing, if it slants to the left the writer is more inhibited. Generally speaking, the farther left the slant is, the more withheld and inhibited the writer.

It is fascinating to see how a person's professional identity or their innermost feelings are revealed in their signature. For example, a tailor might make an "x" in his or her signature look like a pair of scissors; a musician might introduce musical symbols. Similarly, a deeply frustrated or overly erotic person might make the capital "P" resemble parts of the anatomy.

Today I had a great day.

Cynthia Jackson

A signature that is spaced wider than the rest of the writing shows the writer's need for space – to fulfill an urge for self-expansion. Narrow writing depicts a writer who reacts in a reserved or withheld manner, but the wide signature shows that in social circles he artificially likes to show off because this is part of the "social game."

On Monday morning I will be going to Boston to the Tea Party.

Chance Hersey.

A period after a signature points to prudence. If the writer has been subjected to persecution, as in war, he or she tends to be cautious and timid of the world in general. Initial prudence may eventually turn into a personality trait of inherent distrust.

The encircled signature: Picture an embryo protected by an enveloping shield. This indicates a subconscious need to feel secure and less vulnerable. There is a need for privacy, confidentiality and a sense of being protected. If this handwriting is very immature or hard to read, it shows a compensation for earlier aggression. It shows a person who knows that they are aggressive in public and feels the need to curb it. It also can suggest dishonesty. Take the famous case of Jimmy Swaggart, the televangelist. He lost his kingdom of $116 million a year because he had an affair with a hooker. He had an encircled signature. In his case it was a need to hide his cheating from his wife and God.

When the first name appears as only an initial, it means belittlement of self. Usually every person has a first name and a family name. The family is a very important factor in our life and we incorporate its values, relationship and dynamic on a conscious and subconscious level. At times we belittle ourselves at the expense of the more important family. It is like the Mafia's code that the family is more important than the gangster himself. It is not always a great thing: The writer may loose his/her individuality or talent.

17

steven SPIELBERG

Steven Spielberg continues to revolutionize the craft of filmmaking for over three decades. A pioneer in potent psycho-social messages combined with tremendous visual appeal, he ups the industry standard with every new project he creates. As a result, he has countless critically acclaimed credits to his name and a fortune topping $2 billion.

Spielberg dropped out of Cal State Long Beach to pursue his career in film, applying to film school at USC twice, and twice being rejected. To keep in-sync with his passion as a Director, he worked on several television shows but achieved his cinematic breakthrough with "Jaws" in 1975. After that, there was no stopping Spielberg who went on to create and direct some of the biggest and most respected films in the world including: the "Indiana Jones" series, "Close Encounters," "Poltergeist," "E.T.," "Jurassic Park," "Saving Private Ryan," "Schindler's List," to name just a few.

In his films, Spielberg often portrays fathers as reluctant or absent, and shows children, often with divorced parents, and in some sort of danger. He can't resist indulging in galloping fantasy and adventure with a strong dose of morality.

In addition to winning a number of awards within the Film industry, Spielberg has been recognized by Germany, honored with the prestigious "Bundesverdienstkreuz" for "Schindler's List," and was also knighted by Queen Elizabeth II of England, in 2001. He now serves on the board at the USC School of Cinema. Audiences all over the world continue to look to Spielberg to pave the way for state-of-the-art cinema for years to come.

the handwriting reveals:

- Tendency to seek control.

- This highly articulate personality can inject spirituality into the down-to-earth practical side of his accomplishments.

- Tendency to be emotionally volatile. May lead to paying attention to the slightest detail.

- Handwriting of spiritual quality. This may explain his choice of themes.

He applied twice to the USC School of Cinema and was turned down.

1. The simplicity of his **"S"** reveals someone with refined tastes.

2. The looped **"t"** indicates a high sensitivity to interpersonal issues as well as a high degree of creativity.

3. The large loop in the **"g"** indicates a high sexual drive.

4. The overreaching **"l"** and **"b"** suggest that he is very spiritual and craves things beyond the material world.

5. The full-looped **"p"** is associated with a strong physicality, a need for regular exercise.

6. The way the end stroke of the **"n"** descends implies a very stubborn mind.

7. The long starting and end strokes of the **"B"** indicate a tenacity and determination to see things through to the finish.

8. **"Best Wishes"** doesn't stay on a straight line. This could indicate he is struggling with emotional issues and is trying to maintain control.

Her voice, combined with an uncanny talent and chutzpah, brought her to the pinnacle of success.

1. The **"B"** is under the base line indicating unresolved subconscious issues.

2. The upper part of the **"B"** is smaller then the lower part: reveals a strong practical side.

3. A simplified **"S"** shows she is very cultured and possesses good taste.

4. A very long **"t"** cross bar: suggests a powerful, domineering personality with strong leadership qualities.

5. A hook on the right of the **"t"** bar indicates that there is a great deal of determination.

6. The **"a"** is very narrow and knotted: tendency to be secretive and reserved.

7. The space between the lower loop and the stem of the **"B"** indicates a talkative person, a big schmoozer.

barbara STREISAND

Barbara Streisand didn't start out as the beautiful, poised musical and acting genius she is today. Streisand grew up in Brooklyn with an acute sense of loss. Her father died when she was a toddler and she never managed to get along with her stepfather. To escape, young Streisand took refuge in the local movie theaters, dreaming of being an actress.

After high school she moved from Brooklyn to Manhattan to break into theater where her astonishing voice, combined with her chutzpah, took her straight to the top. She began as a regular singer at the Bon Soir nightclub where her act became legendary, attracting fans and industry legends by the dozens each night. She's gone down in history for having won her first Tony award for a debut performance on Broadway in, "I Can Get It for You Wholesale," and it wasn't long before she became one of showbusiness' most prolific performers.

the handwriting reveals:

- Tends to be shy about revealing her inner self and facing social events.

- Very intense personality, with a great deal of tenacity.

- Action-oriented with a lot of ambition.

- Assertive, with a powerful authoritative personality and relentless in pursuing her goals.

adam SANDLER

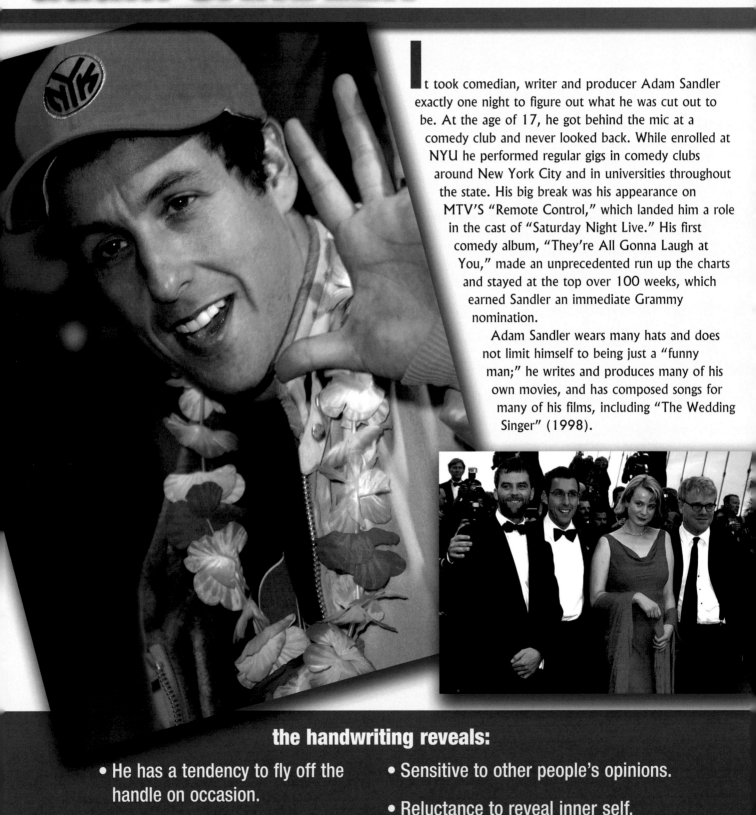

It took comedian, writer and producer Adam Sandler exactly one night to figure out what he was cut out to be. At the age of 17, he got behind the mic at a comedy club and never looked back. While enrolled at NYU he performed regular gigs in comedy clubs around New York City and in universities throughout the state. His big break was his appearance on MTV'S "Remote Control," which landed him a role in the cast of "Saturday Night Live." His first comedy album, "They're All Gonna Laugh at You," made an unprecedented run up the charts and stayed at the top over 100 weeks, which earned Sandler an immediate Grammy nomination.

Adam Sandler wears many hats and does not limit himself to being just a "funny man;" he writes and produces many of his own movies, and has composed songs for many of his films, including "The Wedding Singer" (1998).

the handwriting reveals:

- He has a tendency to fly off the handle on occasion.

- He is goofy.

- Sensitive to other people's opinions.

- Reluctance to reveal inner self.

At 17, he got behind the microphone at a comedy club and never looked back.

1. The **"A"** is open, showing a talkative communicator.

2. The **"m"** is flattened, indicating an evasiveness of some sort and attempts to avoid confrontations.

3. The **"d"** has a tall loopy, stem, meaning a very emotional nature and a love of singing.

4. The **"S"** is like the number 8, indicating a very creative personality.

5. This signature indicates a very dynamic personality with a restless mind; a person who is constantly working on new ventures. In addition, it shows shyness.

History of the Jews

A brief introduction

As we know from the Old Testament, Judaism began with Abraham in 1812 BC. God blessed Abraham and promised to greatly increase his offspring in exchange for eternal worship; the birth of monotheism. Abraham produced two sons; Isaac and Ishmael. Ishmael was the forefather of the Arabs while Isaac, the forefather of the Jews, fathered Jacob, whose sons gave rise to the 12 tribes of Israel. One of them was Joseph, whose brothers sold him around 1544 BC as a slave to Egypt. The Jews had been and remained slaves in Egypt until 1312 BC, when Moses, adopted by the Pharaoh as a baby, by the hand of God, was able to lead the Jews out of bondage. It was on their journey back to the Promised Land, when Moses went up to Mount Sinai, where God delivered the Torah and the Ten Commandments to the Jews, and on they went to the land of Canaan, known now as the land of Israel; the nation of the Jews.

The Early Days of Israel

The Jews were first governed by Judges, set up by Samuel and other holy leaders of the time. Samuel soon anointed Saul, by the selection of God as King of Israel, to be succeeded by the great King David in 877 BC after Saul was killed in battle by the Philistines. King Solomon continued his father's legacy and his pursuit of lofty and noble goals, beginning in 836 BC, and built the First Temple in Jerusalem. In 422 BC the Babylonians conquered Israel, took its people captive, and destroyed the Temple. The Jews were in exile until 370 BC, and at that time started to rebuild the Temple and nourish their culture, trades and overall lives, and Israel flourished.

Freedom didn't last for too long, as in 312 BC the Greeks conquered Israel and would rule for quite some time. In 167 the Maccabees revolted against the Greeks and the miracle of Hanukkah occurred. The oil in the Holy Temple lasted a remarkable eight days instead of one, hence the eight-day celebration of the festival of lights; Hanukkah.

In 63 BC, the Romans had conquered much of the known world and ruled the Jews until 324 AD. The ministry of Jesus, which took place between 27 to 31 AD, inspired people from all over the region to rejoice in life, their fellow man and follow their hearts. As we also know, from the writings and Gospels of the New Testament, it was also a very tumultuous time that would forever change the world.

In 120 AD there was a colossal rebellion of Bar Kocheva against the Roman Empire which resulted in the Romans leveling Jerusalem, destroying the Temple and driving the Jews from Israel once again. By 638 the Moslems had taken over Jerusalem.

Finding their way, again and again; A people without a land of their own.

By the fifth century, Jews had scattered and made new homes throughout Europe and the Middle East. In 1040, one of the greatest interpreters of the Jewish faith, Rashi,

"Your descendants will be like the dust of the earth, and you will spread out to the west and to the east, to the north and to the south. All peoples on earth will be blessed through you and your offspring. I am with you and will watch over you wherever you go, and I will bring you back to this land."

Genesis 28:14-15

began teaching and writing, followed by Maimonides in 1135. The Crusades, which were occurring at the same time, stirred anti-Semitism in medieval Europe. In 1144 the first "blood libel" rumors started spreading, which accused Jews of murdering Christian children and drinking their blood. During 1348 the Black Plague destroyed millions of lives. The Jews were blamed for the spread of the disease.

In 1478 The Catholic Inquisition began, which culminated with the expulsion of the Jews from Spain and Portugal to all parts of Europe, Asia, Africa and so on. It wasn't but 20 years later that Christopher Columbus, with the help of a good number of Jews in Portugal and Spain, discovered America. The era that followed, as the 16th century began, brought rise to the Kabalah in Europe, a mystical tradition that persists to this day. In 1648 the Jews suffered giant massacres led by Chmielinichi in Eastern Europe and by 1654 the first Jews arrived in America.

Anti-Semitism persisted in Europe from the Middle Ages until this very day, sometimes unmistakable, through violence and evident societal restrictions and persecutions, sometimes just under the surface. A late 19th century example was the Dreyfus affair in France, where a Jewish intelligence officer in the French army was wrongly accused of treason and selling secrets to the Germans. Although the allegations were unfounded, anti-Semitic feelings began to spread throughout France, Germany and other parts of Europe where anti-Jewish preaching became so prolific that it was daily routine.

In 1897 the first Zionist congress came together to create a homeland for Jews in Palestine to reestablish the land of Israel that they had been driven out of time and time again. The Balfour Declaration of 1917 launched the attempt by the British to oversee a peaceful settlement of Jews in their Holy Land. But arguments, misunderstandings and severe differences of opinion unleashed wars, big and small between Jews and Arabs, each with a different vision, and by the beginning of World War II, the British had cut immigration to Palestine down to so little that hardly any Jews were being allowed into any country at the time.

In 1933 Hitler came to power in Germany and by 1942, had declared his plans for "the final solution," the eradication of the Jews from the world; an all out plan for genocide. By the end of World War II, six million Jews, along with six million non-Jews, were killed in Nazi concentration camps, yet the Jews surged forward, and ignited what hope and fire they had left in their souls.

By the end of World War II, when the full extent of the Holocaust became public knowledge, Jews were allowed to immigrate to Palestine and they did so in masses. Eventually, the UN took over the mandate of the area from the British, and by 1948, the State of Israel was founded fulfilling God's ancient promise to the Israelites and delivering the Promised Land.

"And Moses turned and went down from the mount, and the two tables of the testimony where in his hand."

Exodus 32:15

sarah jessica PARKER

Sarah Jessica Parker's parents aided their daughter in the launch of her career as a child actor along with several of her eight siblings. Trained in singing and ballet, she earned a role in the Broadway production of "The Innocents" and later in "The Sound of Music," along with four of her brothers and sisters. Her biggest break, by far, was landing the lead in the Broadway run of "Annie," which put her on the map. She stayed in the role for 12 months until she outgrew the rags of Little Orphan Annie.

Rather than enrolling in college, she decided to pursue acting full-time and started out on her movie career. Her talent matured in the early 90s with roles opposite Nicholas Cage in "Honeymoon in Vegas," and "Ed Wood." Today she is best known for her part in the highly-rated and controversial HBO series "Sex and the City." Before marrying Matthew Broderick, Sarah dated Robert Downey Jr., and the late John F. Kennedy Jr.

the handwriting reveals:

- She is extremely outgoing and needs to communicate with other people.

- Strong need to be the center of attention.

- May have difficulties in relationships due to excessive rigidity.

- Very calculated and often practical person.

Best known for her part in the highly-rated and controversial HBO series "Sex and the City," and started her career as Little Orphan Annie.

1. The **"S"** looks like the number 8, suggesting a good mathematical ability and also a strong materialistic side.

2. The **"r"** looks like "1" meaning a very perceptive, probing mind.

3. The **"i"** has a dot behind the letter, suggesting a procrastinator.

4. A very high **"P"** suggests a tendency for pride and vanity.

5. The **"r"** is like a thread, indicating some diplomatic tendencies. May not always be upfront with feelings. May be changeable.

6. The space between **"P"** and **"a"** indicates an ability to wait before reacting.

7. The **"J"** only has a lower zone, meaning a practical and self-reliant personality.

love -
Sarah Jessica Park

"I should have been a doctor. In what other profession can a man tell a woman to take off her clothes and send the bill to her husband?"

1. The **"B"** beginning stroke is curled meaning a tendency for erotic fantasies.

2. The **"B"** upper loop shows a tendency to have vulgar taste, speak profanely and add elaborate touches to simple tasks.

3. The **"t"** cross bar crosses the middle of the stem and curves upwards – action oriented, high aspirations and ambitions. Great deal of imagination and sense of optimism. Assertive personality with plans for success. Highly motivated and compelling. The concave shape is indicative of a sense of humor.

4. The **"J"** upper loop is pointed and looks like a "4" implying problems seeing other points of view.

5. The **"k"** is tall with a full upper stroke indicating a strong sense of humor and a very verbal personality.

6. The **"n"** end stroke curls upward, suggesting a need to protect a sensitive ego.

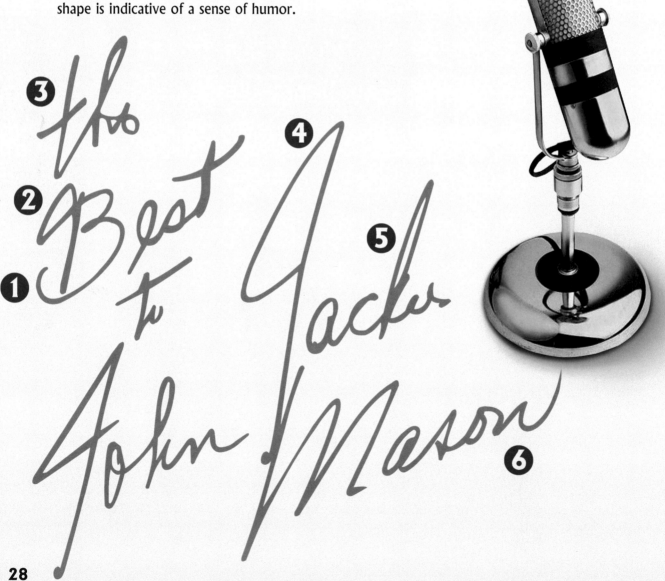

jackie MASON

Jackie Mason was born into a family of rabbis in 1931 in Sheboygan, Wisconsin, and raised on the Lower East Side of Manhattan. He was ordained as a rabbi at the age of 25, but quit three years later in order to pursue stand-up comedy. He performed as a comedian for many years, and made a fateful appearance on "The Ed Sullivan Show," which set his career back: Ed thought Mason had made a crude gesture during the show. He was also blackballed in Hollywood during the McCarthy Era. By 1984 he made a comeback; he won a Tony and an Emmy for his sell-out one-man Broadway show, "The World According to Me."

He is well known for his impersonations of personalities like Richard Nixon and Ronald Reagan and performed for Queen Elizabeth II in 1991. Among his memorable lines are: "I should have been a doctor. In what other profession can a man tell a woman to take off her clothes and send the bill to her husband?"

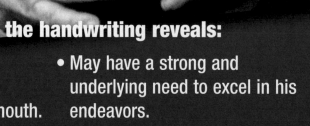

the handwriting reveals:

• Quick-witted with a colorful personality: whatever is on this writer's mind comes out of his mouth.

• Razor sharp and critical in his approach to his work.

• May have a strong and underlying need to excel in his endeavors.

• May find it difficult to accept authority.

ben STILLER

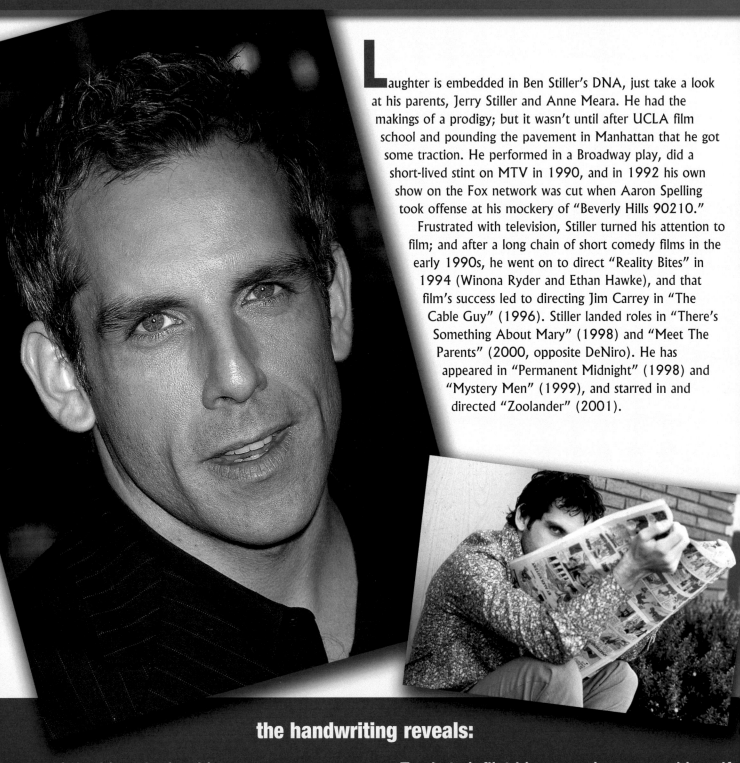

Laughter is embedded in Ben Stiller's DNA, just take a look at his parents, Jerry Stiller and Anne Meara. He had the makings of a prodigy; but it wasn't until after UCLA film school and pounding the pavement in Manhattan that he got some traction. He performed in a Broadway play, did a short-lived stint on MTV in 1990, and in 1992 his own show on the Fox network was cut when Aaron Spelling took offense at his mockery of "Beverly Hills 90210." Frustrated with television, Stiller turned his attention to film; and after a long chain of short comedy films in the early 1990s, he went on to direct "Reality Bites" in 1994 (Winona Ryder and Ethan Hawke), and that film's success led to directing Jim Carrey in "The Cable Guy" (1996). Stiller landed roles in "There's Something About Mary" (1998) and "Meet The Parents" (2000, opposite DeNiro). He has appeared in "Permanent Midnight" (1998) and "Mystery Men" (1999), and starred in and directed "Zoolander" (2001).

the handwriting reveals:

• Little things bother him.

• May appear odd; and he may not always be easily understood by other people.

• Tends to inflict his own misery upon himself.

• Tendency to be controversial and underhanded.

Laughter is embedded in Ben Stiller's DNA, just take a look at his parents…

1. The **"B"** opens at the bottom, indicating a very talkative personality, with a somewhat inflated ego.

2. The flattened **"n"** suggests changeability and the ability to be diplomatic.

3. The **"i"** is short and straight implying a clear mind, good organizing ability.

4. The **"l"** is straight and simplified showing a quick mind and good grasp of essentials.

5. The shape of the **"er"** shows a probing mind and a tendency towards sarcasm.

6. The **"S"** with small hooks – indicates persistence.

7. The **"n"** end stroke going backwards suggests a capacity for self-deprecation.

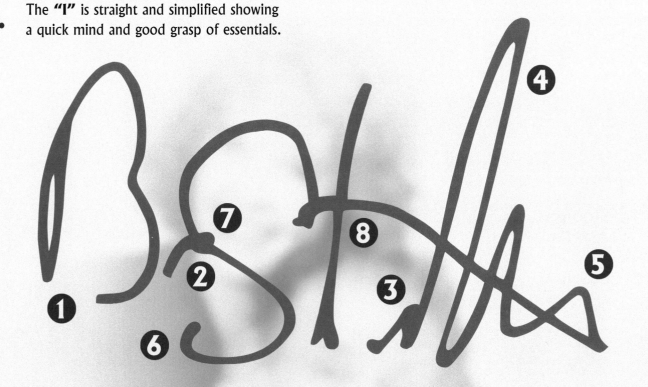

personal PRONOUN "I"

The Copy Book "I" (The textbook "I" that is taught in school): The Copy Book "I" is usually a positive sign. The writer tends to conform to societal rules and prefers not to stand out in a crowd. The writer is also conventional. He or she has experienced parental love and guidance and therefore respects authority and social norms.

On Saturday afternoon, I will be going to Dillards.

Jennifer E Rother

The Stick-like "I": This person is independent, direct, and straightforward – free from conventional societal demands, and is not hurt by slights or insults. The writer likes to think of himself as "Numero Uno." Usually this person is more likely to judge situations objectively rather than superimpose his own emotional agenda on them.

On Saturday afternoon I will be going to Dillards.

Roman numeral "I": This person has self-confidence. She is creative, independent and cultured. She has a strong mental energy and can create conclusions and concepts from the events around her. She also tends to have an inquisitive mind that penetrates into her surroundings.

On Tuesday afternoon, I will be

The "I" like a Roman numeral, but curved on top: Think of an umbrella that protects you on a rainy day. This writer has warmth and tenderness based on his relationship with his father. Also look for humor in the relationships of this person.

Father → I ← Mother

The Father/Mother "I": The Personal Pronoun "I" has two parts which indicate the subconscious attitude of the writer towards his relationships with his parents. The horizontal extension reflects the attitude towards his father, while the vertical loop reflects his feelings towards his mother. When either of these parts are missing or distorted it is a sure sign of a psychological glitch within his relationship with the respective parent.

On Friday morning I will

A Round "I": Shows a nurturing and self-satisfied person. She tends to be a caregiver and warm, and can be expected to be peaceful much of the time. However, if the rest of the handwriting is illegible then the Round "I" becomes a negative indicator of a "me-first" attitude.

The personal pronoun "I" is the only word in English that has one letter. It is a very important tool in the hand of psychologists. It encompasses and contains the past, the present and future of the person. It is the one letter that we identify as our own personality, or ego, just as body language reflects our personality. We write it automatically and unconsciously that way.

Ida and I are going to

The "I" is over blown: This denotes protective and maternal instincts, an emotionally effusive and protective caregiver. The writer is very supportive of the people around him and provides an environment that nurtures free expression of ideas and actions. He tolerates opposing ideas without experiencing anxiety.

On friday afternoon I wil

The angular "I": This shows some aggression, hostility and spite. It might be a result of anxiety and fear implemented by an over demanding father and probably an unhappy early childhood. Aggression was accepted and tolerated in his home during the formative years.

I

The "I" that is pointed at the top: Indicates a penetrating mind. The writer likes to get to the bottom of what is happening around him or her. They like to view all of the facts before they render judgement or a course of action. They don't like ambiguous thinking or behavior, they call a spade, a spade.

In grade school 2 was very

The "I" that looks like the number 2: The writer either has a number aptitude or is someone who craves security and feels second-class; this writer could have a somewhat defensive personality.

Ida and I, are

The "I" has what looks like a claw to the left: This is usually a negative indicator. The claw symbolizes an attack on some hurtful inner residue from the past. It is also found that many criminals write their "I" in this way, hence it is called the "felon claw."

♪

The "I" like a musical symbol: This writer has musical interests and abilities, or subconsciously identifies with them. Throughout the world of graphology we see again and again that the main occupation of the writer is reflected in one of the letters. For example, a famous soccer player wrote the Hebrew letter "nun" to resemble a leg kicking a ball.

She has a steamy sexuality, and a smart, tough sense of independence.

1. An extended **"L"** shows that she has an extremely positive and optimistic outlook, plus a pride in her bearing that becomes her.

2. The looped **"B"** shows a high level of imagination that includes the erotic.

3. The Roman **"e"** denotes quite a cultured personality.

4. The **"t"** looks like a hook: She is able to exert pressure on herself and others to reach her goals and fulfill her own needs.

5. The capital **"A"** is square and has a curved stroke, indicating some mechanical abilities combined with a great deal of sensitivity and dislike for interference in her affairs.

6. A very long **"y"** loop suggests a strong need to explore the subconscious and a strong need for intimacy.

7. The **"s"** is looped, indicating a tendency to be defensive.

8. A very long end stroke indicates that she likes to express her freedom.

9. A double-looped **"a"** implies a tendency to tell white lies.

lauren BACALL

In 1943, filmmaker Howard Hawks was looking for a new face to cast when his wife showed him the cover of an issue of Harper's Bazaar with the photograph of a striking model. She was a nice Jewish girl named Betty Joan Perske. Hawks knew immediately that she was what he was looking for, and signed her to a seven-year contract. He changed her name and cast her opposite Humphrey Bogart in "To Have and Have Not" (1944) which gave birth to one of the most legendary romances in Hollywood history.

Bacall and Bogart married in 1945 and appeared in three other films together: "The Big Sleep" (1946), "Dark Passage" (1947), and "Key Largo" (1948). She won over audiences with her steamy sexuality, underpinned by a smart, tough independence. After caring for Bogart until his death of cancer in 1957, she turned partly to the stage. She won Tony awards for her roles in the Broadway musical "Applause" (1970) and "Woman of the Year" (1981) and was nominated for an Academy Award for her role as Barbara Streisand's sharp-tongued mother in "The Mirror Has Two Faces" (1996).

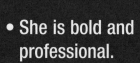

HUMPHREY BOGART
USA 32

- She is bold and professional.

- Tendency to be flirtatious.

the handwriting reveals:

- Can be rigid.

- Altogether very artistic and distinctive, full of resourceful ideas.

billy CRYSTAL

Billy's paternal grandfather was a Yiddish actor. His mother loved the theater and performed in shows at the synagogue. Crystal's father invited jazz musicians to the family home on a regular basis, where Billy met Billie Holiday, W.C. Handy, and other jazz legends. He entertained his family by learning "jive" and impersonating comedians. He majored in theater and studied TV and film directing under Martin Scorsese; but comedy was always his shtick: He co-founded a three-person improv troupe that got gigs in night clubs and on TV.

His big break came after moving to Los Angeles, when Norman Lear spotted him at the Comedy Store and Crystal's talent was unleashed via a series of character roles: first, in "All In The Family;" then, as the first openly homosexual character in the history of television, and then as the first pregnant man on TV. Hollywood then picked him up, and Billy Crystal stands today as one of the most sought-after comedians in the business. He has hosted the Academy Awards a number of times, to high acclaim.

the handwriting reveals:

- Has a strong sense of humor with sharp, intense personality.

- Down to earth.

- An extremely sensual person who likes the goodies that life has to offer.

- Strong sense of belonging and a need to connect to his roots.

He keeps the world laughing and added pizzazz to the title Master of Ceremonies for the Oscars.

1. The **"B"** is hooked, indicating a preoccupation with subconscious material.

2. The **"B"** has no upper loop: a very sharp mind with a highly tuned sense of humor.

3. The **"i"** dot is a dash: he pokes fun at himself.

4. The **"y"** end stroke is short, suggesting the ability to sublimate basic needs.

5. The **"t"** cross bar return indicates a high level of tenacity. Tends to be very sensitive to criticism.

6. The **"r"** pointed pick on the first stroke denotes curiosity and a critical nature.

7. The **"C"** is very hooked, implying a difficulty to let go of psychological material that hurts the writer.

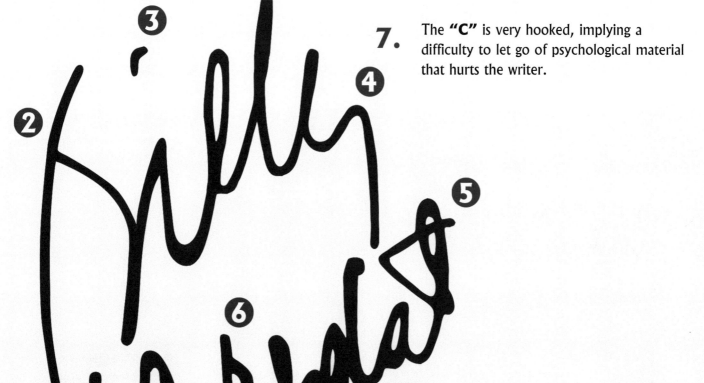

The man who brought Hitler to Broadway: his comedies are usually wild parodies that mix satire with slapstick.

1. The end stroke of the final **"s"** in the name "Brooks" reveals a person who, when provoked, is not afraid to fight back.

2. The small, sharp connections in the name "Brooks" indicate a person who is articulate and possessed of a sharp tongue.

3. While the use of an exclamation point in normal writing is common, it is quite rare to use exclamation points in an autograph. Use of the exclamation point reveals a writer's forceful personality and can suggest his need to be the one in charge.

4. The fact that the capital first letters are disconnected from the words they initiate shows a capacity to observe and to pause before action.

5. In Mel Brooks' writing the **"t"** cross bar is very optimistic (it goes up) and also practical because it's toward the middle of the stem.

6. The low middle hump of the capital **"M"** indicates dissatisfaction over social inequality.

7. Capital **"M"** (first hump): indicates an ambitious person.

8. The looping way he writes his **"B's"** and **"A"** indicate a great deal of sensitivity and imagination.

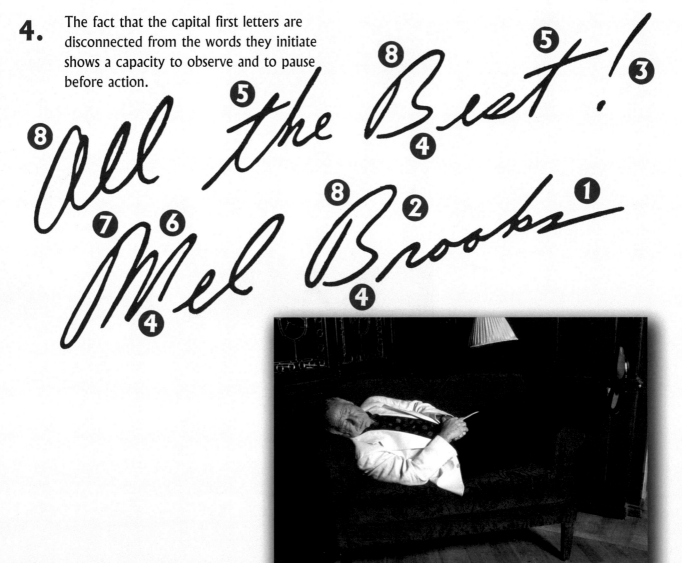

mel BROOKS

Brooks launched his career in comedy doing stand-up in a string of resorts in the Catskills after World War II. He soon shifted to writing for Sid Caesar's "Your Show of Shows" in the early 50s. Later, in 1964, he collaborated with Carl Reiner on the classic stand-up routine "The 2,000-Year-Old Man," some of the best developed characters in comedy to this day.

Turning to film, Brooks wrote and directed "The Producers" (1968), a comedic masterpiece of uproarious bad taste. His other hit comedies are usually wild parodies that mix satire with slapstick; they include "Blazing Saddles" (1974), a spoof of Western movies; and "High Anxiety" (1977), a comic version of an Alfred Hitchcock classic. He collaborated with Thomas Meehan to turn "The Producers" into a Broadway musical in 2000. The show went on to win 15 Tony Awards.

Mel Brooks' production company, Brooksfilms, has given us a notable pastiche of films, a few being: "The Elephant Man" (1980), "Frances" (1982), and "84 Charing Cross Road" (1986), for which wife Anne Bancroft received the British Academy Award opposite Anthony Hopkins.

the handwriting reveals:

- Is quiet and shy at times.

- A very sharp personality with the tenacity to fight for his ideas; unwilling to give up under pressure.

- He has the right mixture of a great, creative mind on the one hand, as well as the ability to carry out what his imagination visualizes.

- Overall high-strung with a tendency for self-indulgence.

michael DOUGLAS

This eldest son of the legendary Kirk Douglas came to acting reluctantly when forced to pick a major at UC Santa Barbara. He began working painfully at it, and when his father went to see his first college performance, he said Michael was terrible. Little did he know at that time he had another rising star in the family. Michael soon nurtured his talents and became a legitimate double threat, with a track record for selling movies unrivaled by any of his actor/producer peers.

Douglas was little more than a blip on the radar screen when he hit a home run producing "One Flew over the Cuckoo's Nest (1975)," which brought in runaway box office returns and a sweep of the top five Oscars. Until "Romancing The Stone (1984)," Douglas was more highly regarded as a producer than an actor, but his role in "Romancing The Stone," would change that forever. Michael Douglas has been one of the top 10 box office stars since that day and has achieved high acclaim and respect for his craft to this very day. Today Douglas is married to the beautiful actress Katherine Zeta Jones, and is a proud father.

the handwriting reveals:

• Constantly tries to stabilize inner turbulence.

• Tendency not to forget who crosses his path. Can be vindictive.

• Extremely analytical and detail-oriented.

• A person who constantly wrestles with inner intellectual chaos.

His father, Kirk, once called Michael a "terrible" actor. It's a good thing he was proven wrong.

1. The **"f"** shows family achievements are very important.

2. The first hump of the **"M"** is very tall, suggesting an ambitious personality with a very high opinion of himself.

3. The **"I"** has a back claw suggesting the use of guilt to punish others. It can also mean negativity.

4. The **"i"** dot is very high: this writer strives intellectually to find answers, is idealistic and ambitious. He likes to think in terms of possibilities.

5. The **"g"** looks like a stick, suggesting strong sexual energy and restlessness due to unresolved subconscious issues.

He approached every role with great intensity.

1. The **"K"** loops left, suggesting a need to protect his sensitive ego.

2. The **"I"** is a straight line indicating a simple, no-nonsense personality.

3. The **"D"** is open with a wide loop: a creative and talkative personality.

4. The **"e"** has an inner loop indicating a person who hangs on to ideas.

5. The **"t"** stem is full and hooked to the right, indicating a mixture of sensitivity, anger and frustration.

6. The **"g"** is long and straight. This is associated with strong physical needs.

7. The **"i"** dot dashed to the right signifies a sharp minded personality. Sometimes tends to turn aggression against self.

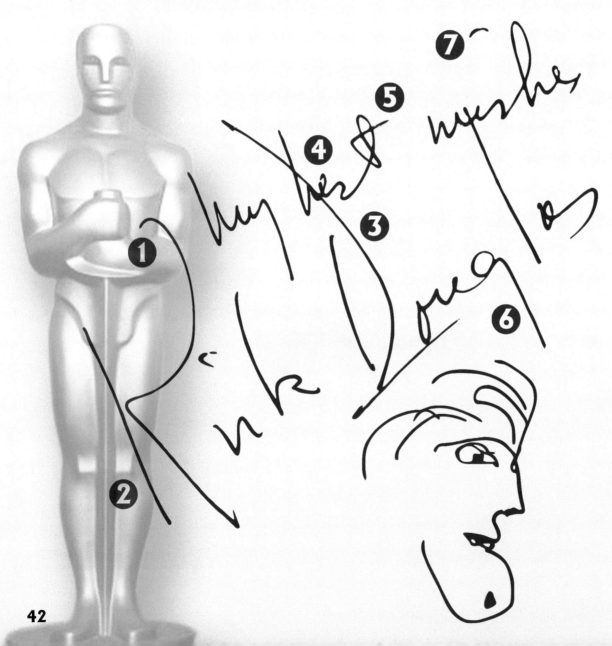

kirk DOUGLAS

Born Issur Danielovitch in 1916, this talented young man grew up in poverty in upstate New York. He was famous for saying, "there's nowhere to go but up." Young Issur worked his way through college as a waiter, and managed to parlay a strong athletic body, handsome face (with the famous cleft chin), and a powerful voice into an acting career that brought him fame and fortune far beyond his father's modest dreams of success.

Kirk Douglas has approached every role with an intensity that sometimes bordered on hysteria, and has a driven quality most evident in the way he plays his characters: a corrupt newspaperman in "Ace in the Hole" (1951), an ambitious movie producer in "The Bad and the Beautiful" (1952), Van Gogh in "Lust for Life" (1955). He has nearly 100 films to his credit. He is a great supporter of Israel and played the Jewish hero Colonel Mickey Marcus in the 1966 film "Cast a Giant Shadow." Sadly, he suffered a debilitating stroke in 1995. He celebrated his Bar Mitzvah the second time when he was 83.

the handwriting reveals:

- A highly driven personality.
- A strong sense of integrity and honesty.
- A sense of mystery.
- Spiritual aspirations.

Jews in Hollywood

One of the most frequent maxims of anti-Semitism is that the Jews control the media and, in particular, Hollywood. Well, it's not altogether untrue. Most of the moguls are still Jewish, although, as Ben Stein points out, there are a lot more gentiles in positions of power now. Hollywood has come to symbolize glamour, glory, show biz, shallowness, trend-setting, scandals, creativity, legends, and, above all, Manna for the millions. It has power beyond any other propaganda tool.

It is true, Jews did create Hollywood, just as they became the trendsetters during the Golden Age in Spain or in Moslem Europe, or even during their slavery in Egypt, when their population burgeoned.

The fathers of Hollywood include the founders of the most well-known studios:

- Universal Pictures was founded by German Jew, Carl Laemmle, who was born in a small village in Germany and fled the poverty of his home town to come to America.

- Paramount Pictures was created by Hungarian Jew, Adolph Zucker. He was orphaned as a small child and came to America lonely and rejected.

- Fox Film Corporation – again we see a Hungarian Jew, William Fox, who came to the US as a poor immigrant selling soda and sandwiches and worked as a chimney sweeper.

- Metro-Goldwyn-Mayer was created by Louis B. Mayer, who was born in Russia and fled his father's junkyard business to build the greatest studio of all.

- Warner Brothers – Benjamin Warner, an ambitious Jewish boy, came from Poland to seek his fortune. Once settled in the United States he worked as a cobbler in Baltimore, peddled notions from a wagon, and tried to eke out a living so that he could feed his four sons: Harry, Sam, Albert, and Jack. Then he bought a broken movie projector and the rest is history.

Hollywood represents another saga of the Jews, which repeats itself in every country and every century; people coming from nowhere and reaching the pinnacle of success from the bottom of the barrel. So many of these Jews mentioned, and those who we haven't even introduced, came from backgrounds of failure and suffering. For so many years, many of these people had lost one or both of their parents, mainly their fathers. In cases where there were two parents at home, the turmoil of the times had made men bitter, good-for-nothing, so to speak, and failing at careers in their homelands.

One could say the success in Hollywood for these men was derived from a psychological need to escape their fathers' fate, their European roots, the language and accent barriers, the customs and the religious persecution. However, from archetypal point of view, one can never run away from one's ancestry or oneself. These accomplishments remind us of the story of Joseph, who came to Egypt as a slave and ended up the right-hand-man of the Pharaoh.

Jews produced the very first movie, "Cohen's Advertising Scheme," and the first American feature film was "The Great Train Robbery" (1903), starring a very illustrious and very Jewish actor/writer/director by the name of Max Anderson. He wrote and directed many other westerns for years to come. The first "talkie" was created by Warner Brothers, a story about a Jewish boy who rejects the wishes of his father to become a cantor and instead becomes a star; Al Jolson as "The Jazz Singer."

The Jews also launched the independent studio system. David O. Selznick produced "Gone with the Wind" in 1939, Hal Roach made the "Laurel and Hardy" films, and Sam Spiegel created "The African Queen," "On the Waterfront," and "Lawrence of Arabia."

To this very day, Jews continue to lead the way, with their Jewish and non-Jewish counterparts in the film industry. Steven Spielberg and Woody Allen are among the most well-known and most respected trendsetting directors in the world.

The brilliance, talent, and genius of the Jews, in founding Hollywood, spread the image of America all over the world. They continue to do so, and not because of any conspiracy, simply because of their appreciation to America for their acceptance and because success just happened to be "in their blood."

1. The **"W"** is closed, suggesting a very ambitious personality.

2. The **"b"** is angular, showing a very aggressive mind.

3. The **"t"** cross bar is sharp on the left, indicating a tendency for bad temper and possible aggressiveness.

4. The **"y"** has a long, straight stem, revealing great intensity and ability to concentrate. This writer values privacy and can work alone very well.

5. The **"er"** is like thread, implying diplomacy and perhaps evasiveness.

6. The **"R"** is very high, indicating an insistence on having one's own way.

winona RYDER

At the age of seven, Winona Horowitz, and her counterculture family from Minnesota moved to an upscale commune in Northern California. Her godfather was LSD guru Timothy Leary. She began acting lessons at age 10 in San Francisco, and at 13 began her film career. She changed her name before her starring role in Tim Burton's "Beetlejuice." (1988).

She later latched onto a promising screenplay based on Bram Stoker's novel, Dracula. She appeared in a series of movies in the early 90s, and was nominated for a Best Actress Oscar for her portrayal of Jo in "Little Women" (1994). She starred in and was the executive producer of "Girl, Interrupted."

Late in 2001 Ryder was arrested for shoplifting. This led the court to charge her with misdemeanor in 2004.

the handwriting reveals:

- The handwriting shows that she may have an aggressive side.

- A somewhat odd personality who sometimes takes unusual twists when viewing reality.

- Tendency to display strange behavior, possibly the result of unfinished business in the subconscious.

- High intelligence with strong intellectual tendencies.

milton BERLE

"**U**ncle Miltie," also known as "Mr. Television," was a child actor who began performing on the stage at age 5 in 1913 and in films like, "The Perils of Pauline," just a few years later. Encouraged by his stage mother from the start, his career spanned 88 years, during which he published more than 400 songs. Berle appeared on Broadway for 30 years beginning in his teens, but it was "The Texaco Star Theatre" that earned him a 30-year contract with NBC.

"Uncle Miltie," had America glued to the TV set every Tuesday night, doing anything for a laugh, which he always got. He would always come out on stage in a shocking costume, sometimes in drag.

He was also known as a "gag thief;" he joked about how well he stole other comedians' lines.

He also appeared in a number of films, and wrote a two-volume autobiography, plus a compendium of jokes. "That's the important part of my life, making people laugh," he once said.

the handwriting reveals:

- Strong, private side.

- Cultivated and secretive.

- Could be very arrogant, belligerent, rowdy, and could appear aggressive to outsiders.

- Underneath the mask of arrogance was a totally different personality.

"Uncle Miltie," Mr. Television himself; a Jewish comedian who raised the Shtick bar to the highest...

1. The **"I"** tilts to the left, indicating a subconscious need to protect a sensitive ego.

2. The **"I"** is also rounded: The writer needed a great deal of attention, admiration and love.

3. The over-pumped **"A"** indicates a person who was emotionally extroverted, somewhat intense at times.

4. The **"m"** looks like thread, meaning the writer could be a diplomat and avoid arguments. It also can mean that he did not always tell the truth.

5. The beginning stroke of the **"M"** indicates a great sense of humor.

6. The first hump in the **"M"** is higher, which shows a very ambitious personality.

7. The **"t"** cross bar tilted downward means stubbornness.

8. The **"B"** is like the number 8 – a sign for a very creative personality.

Mr. Television

The man who altered the face of television comedy forever started out his career in public relations, but in 1950, he found his true calling.

1. The gap in the **"N"** indicates someone who is intuitive and a quick thinker who subconsciously doesn't want to be connected to the past.

2. The **"N"** is very looped in the beginning stroke, indicating a tendency to be jealous.

3. The **"o"** with the inner loop ending upward suggests a quick, high-flying mind.

4. Very high end stroke means a person who can get highly ambitious projects done.

5. The **"m"** is toothed and angular, indicating an analytical mind and possibly some social aggression.

6. The **"L"** is very high with an upper loop denoting predominance of intellectual interests. The everyday world may be too boring for him.

7. The **"r"** is retraced and angular and ends under the base line, indicating generosity and a need to handle strong emotions through his own experience.

8. Underscored signature implies an assertive and brilliant personality with originality and self-confidence. At times can be aggressive with a forceful temper.

50

norman LEAR

The man who altered the face of television comedy forever started out his career in public relations, but in 1950, he found his true calling. Lear worked as a writer/producer in television throughout the 50s and 60s – then, in the 70s, developed "All in the Family." With that show, he introduced racism, anti-Semitism, abortion and homosexuality to television comedy, with Archie Bunker as the main character, played by legendary actor Carroll O'Conner, a stereotypical working-class bigot from Queens. Word has it the character of Archie Bunker was inspired, in part, by Lear's own father.

After "All in the Family," Lear became known for groundbreaking situation comedies that featured families that regularly confronted major political and social issues of their day. He followed up with "Maude" and "Mary Hartman, Mary Hartman," a brilliant take on soap operas that received prime air time. He has produced and written more than 60 shows throughout his career. Lear has been active in many political causes. He is the winner of numerous awards for his public service and his writing and has been married three times.

the handwriting reveals:

- Not always healthy, with mood swings.

- Highly inspirational person, who can motivate people to perform and do things for him.

- Very unusual personality, one that leaves its mark on people.

- Tendency to integrate political and spiritual ideas into his life.

MATISYAHU

Matisyahu (Hebrew for Matthew) writes and performs music mixing reggae along the lines of traditional Rasta Roots stylings, traditional rap, and guitar solos typical of rock music. Most of his songs are almost entirely in English with just a few words of Hebrew and Yiddish sprinkled in. When Esquire gave him an Esky Music Award in 2006, the magazine called him "the most intriguing reggae artist in the world." That same year he was also named as Top Reggae Artist by Billboard magazine. His single "King without a Crown" reached the No. 7 spot on Billboard's Hot Modern Rock Tracks. He was born as Matthew Paul Miller in West Chester, Pennsylvania, in 1979 and grew up in White Plains, New York, not knowing that at his circumcision ceremony he had been named Feivish Hershel. He became Orthodox around 2001 and has been affiliated with the Lubavitcher Hasidic community in Crown Heights, Brooklyn, New York. He prefers to pray with Stolin-Karlin Hasidim who have the custom of screaming ecstatically when they pray.

the handwriting reveals:

- Moves away from his past, as indicated by the widening left margin.

- Highly intuitive person.

- An emotional person full of enthusiasm.

- An unpretentious person.

"I want my music to have meaning, to be able to touch people and make them think."

1. Precisely dotted **"i"**: when needed the writer knows how to be very precise in his communications.

2. At times the writer can be hasty and looses his patience.

3. Modest and confident.

4. Long **"t"** bar indicates a strong-willed person.

5. This **"s"** suggests a high level of sensitivity and creative ability.

6. Capital in the middle of a sentence: the writer may be somewhat under pressure.

7. High-stemmed **"d"**: idealistic and sincere.

relationships & GRAPHOLOGY

LOWER ZONE – The most important indicator regarding sexuality is the lower zone of the letters "y" and "g." The rationale is that lower zone represents our subconscious and material needs, so that people who have problems around sexuality translate it into the telltale lower zones of those letters.

A short lower zone: The writer has some denial of legitimacy of sexuality. She represses her emotions and consequently is not so invested in the broad sexual experience. The writer might also have a weak libido and sexual insecurity.

Inflated lower zones: This writer has a great money sense – and a very sexual personality. The writer is in great need of bodily pleasures and likes to receive kisses and hugs from those he is close to.

Full, with pressure: This person is very athletic, loves to dance, swim, and jog – is very physical and determined. This leads to great sexual performance.

Hooks in the lower zone: This shows that the writer has many hang-ups around sex because of religious and/or neurotic reasons. The hook indicates someone who might be impotent, unable to complete the sexual act or who has problems with their libido.

The lower zone is a short stick: This writer, like #1 above, doubts the legitimacy of sexuality, or might have a problem expressing emotions. The writer wants immediate satisfaction out of the relationship.

The lower zone forms a long stick: This writer has a strong libido, has sexual fantasies and often is unsatisfied sexually. The writer might also like to explore the subconscious issues at hand and probe into the underlying dynamic between him and his significant other.

Senator Gary Hart, who was in line to win the Democratic nomination – and many other public figures who were brought down because of the allure of sex. Sex, of course, contains all three dimensions of being human: the physical, the emotional and the psychological. And the handwriting can tell a lot about sexual proclivities: Many sex offenders and deviants, for example, can be detected through their script.

PRESSURE – The next factor is the pressure of the pen. As a rule of thumb, the heavier the pressure on the pen (you can feel it by touching the back side of the written paper), the more intense and vigorous is the sexual act.

I are going to

Light pressure: This writer is very lighthearted, likes peace and harmony, and most probably his or her performance of sex is more delicate rather then the passionate, aggressive variety.

On Friday Morning I will

Heavy pressure: Suggests a strong-willed, dynamic person, who experiences sex as a sensual, tactile experience. Vigorous sexual performer with deep emotional memory and the need for plenty of stimulation – therefore, this person can be a demanding sexual partner.

SPACING OF THE WORDS – Another factor of sexual graphology is the togetherness in sex. The most important indicator is the spacing of the words on the line. The spacing of words ranges from a very narrow, intense space to, of course, a wide space. It is measured by computing the ratio of the letter's height to the distance between two words.

A crook is a straight line

Wide space: The person needs his or her personal space; she might go off to read a newspaper after sex. She may frustrate her partner because her partner often feels neglected and abandoned.

---

afternoon I will

Narrow, intense space: The writer is a very intense sexual performer, and is likely to want frequent sex with greater intimacy. At times the partner feels a "lack of oxygen" which might lead to a blow-out.

PASTINESS – Pastiness means the thinness or the thickness of the line. If the line is very thin and sharp, the writer is more genteel and more contained. If the line is thick, heavy and smeared, the person is more sensual. This writer needs more back rubs.

James Gear

A thick line: This writer uses a lot of good imagination in sex, along with vitality, warmth, sensitivity, and touch. The writer enjoys bodily contact, has a strong physical appetite and is sexually adventurous. Many sex offenders have this component in their handwriting. However, the overall quality of the handwriting determines whether it is healthy or pathological.

The list of quirky, successful films turned by Allen is endless, and America never seems to tire of the Woody Allen style of filmmaking.

1. The first name is spaced out, showing an intuitive way of thinking, with creativity.

2. The writing is large with tall end strokes, indicating a personality full of ambition with a subconscious need to protect a sensitive ego in public.

3. The "o" as a double circle, implying a tendency to be evasive at times.

4. A full loop on the "d" suggesting an over emotional personality, with open-mindedness and extreme sensitivity. This writer can be fussy in interpersonal relations and get hurt easily.

5. A short stem on the "y" indicates intense feelings regarding sexuality.

6. The "en" is like thread, again showing a tendency towards evasiveness in interpersonal relationships.

7. The "A" is a circle within a circle. Indicates a person who lives in a world of his own.

56

woody ALLEN

Woody Allen was born Allen Stewart Konigsberg in New York City in 1935 to Orthodox Jewish parents. He briefly attended New York University and then City College of New York, both of which expelled him within a few months due to poor attendance and low marks. He switched from school into his real passion; writing comedy for television. He worked on "The Tonight Show," "The Gary Moore Show," and other programs and was held in high-regard by many in the industry. In the late 1950s he started doing stand-up in Greenwich Village nightclubs, which is usually difficult for a shy man. Through his intellectual and comedic genius, Woody Allen managed to create his now famous persona: An intelligent contemporary urban man struggling feebly against the anxieties of the cold, harsh, modern world.

Following the divorce in 1960 from his first wife, he has married, divorced, and moved in with several famous women, including Mia Farrow, and has been happily married to Soon-Yi Previn since1997. The couple has two children.

The list of quirky, successful films turned by Allen is endless, and America never seems to tire of the Woody Allen style of filmmaking.

the handwriting reveals:

• The writing shows mood swings with high sensitivity.

• Ability to surprise people surprise people with unexpected responses to situations and encounters.

• Secretiveness is quite pronounced in his handwriting.

• Possible Dr. Jeckle and Mr. Hyde-type tendencies.

william SHATNER

Born in Canada, William "Captain Kirk" Shatner started out with a business degree from McGill University; but his own, very different drummer led him to New York City after college to pursue a career in acting. His rugged good looks and stentorian voice made him stand out from the rest, commanding audiences of all kinds. He immediately began working regularly in supporting parts on Broadway and in live television.

Most know Shatner from the hit series "Star Trek," which had its start in 1966; but it wasn't until his third try with "Star Trek" that he became a major star. The third try was "Star Trek: The Motion Picture," in 1979, and the film's sequels. Shortly afterward he earned the starring role on "T.J. Hooker," a crime-drama from which he achieved considerable fame.

He has appeared in over 40 films, and has successfully launched a series of sci-fi books and films. He also has a stake in the internet company Priceline and appears, as radiant as ever, in many of their commercials.

the handwriting reveals:

- A powerful mind with an optimistic view of the world.

- A generous and giving personality eager for social interaction.

- Highly imaginative combining practicality with a need to escape into a fantasy world.

- Subconscious need to protect oneself from critics.

The first "Star Trek" series was a commercial catastrophe; but the original 79 episodes are translated into 47 languages and are on the air more than 200 times a day worldwide.

1. A space between the capital **"W"** and the rest of the first name indicates cautiousness with first-time encounters in social situations.

2. The **"W's"** end stroke is inverted, implying a need for self-protection.

3. The **"i"** dot is very high – highly imaginative with a high level of inspiration.

4. The **"S"** loops at the top, suggesting a person who often gets wrapped up in his own needs.

5. The **"t"** cross bar is long and slants upward suggesting an extremely optimistic and powerful mind. Visionary tendencies with a sense of being able to accomplish whatever he sets his mind on.

6. The **"t"** cross bar is hooked at the end, indicating a person who does not always practice "forgive and forget."

7. The **"r"** ends stroke up suggesting generosity and a very open heart.

8. The **"n"** is square. This writer is mechanically inclined, and gets pleasure out of working with his hands.

9. The two last humps of the **"m"** are lumped together, indicating a tendency to be evasive and diplomatic.

59

Miracles & Jews

Miracles are the fingerprint of God throughout the story of the Bible.

A few of the best known miracles are:

- The rod turning into a serpent during the Exodus, when Moses wanted to prove to the Jews that God was blessing them.

- The signs and wonders performed through Moses, as told in stories of Pesach (Passover) prior to Pharaoh allowing the Jews to leave, among them: the water in the Nile turning into blood and the plague that killed all the first born sons of Egypt.

- The Red Sea dividing to allow the Jews to pass into freedom.

- Manna: the miraculous food from heaven provided by God to the Jews.

- Joshua and the crumbling of the walls of Jericho at the trumpets' blast.

- The slaying of Goliath by David.

"Miracles have become rarer since the destruction of the first Holy Temple. Nevertheless, there have been more glimpses of the supernatural, such as the miracle of Chanukah. For the past 2000 years Jews have lived in exile. Until recently they were banished from their homeland. Some see the creation of modern Israel and the victory in the Six Day War of 1967 as modern day miracles.

Some view Jews as a miraculous people who seemingly possess the ability to steadfastly remain loyal to God throughout thousands of years of persecution.

According to some Jewish philosophies every day is an opportunity for Divine intervention benefiting all humans and other beings as well."

"He rebuked the Red Sea, and it dried up;
he led them through the depths as through a desert.
He saved them from the hand of the foe;
from the hand of the enemy he redeemed them."

Psalm 106:9-10

scientists

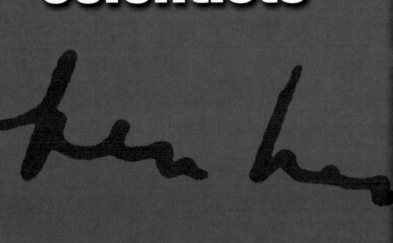

When his predictions based on the theory came true in 1919, it sent shock waves through the world's scientific community and the popular press.

1. The simple capital **"T"** indicates a simple, unpretentious person.

2. The floating cross bar on the **"T"** suggests a person with spiritual depth.

3. The way all the lowercase letters are attached is a sign of a person who strings concepts together in a logical succession.

4. The ascending cross bar in the **"t"** indicates a powerful analytical and ambitious mind.

5. When someone initializes their first name, it can indicate that the writer feels his family is more important than his individual identity.

6. The thick heavy writing means the writer bore down heavily while writing. This is suggestive of a sensual, tactile person.

albert EINSTEIN

This German-Jewish genius who changed the way the world viewed the planet earth and the universe had a discouraging beginning. Although a native to Germany, Einstein trained for four years at the Swiss Polytechnic School in Zurich, Albert Einstein couldn't find a job teaching physics and mathematics. He resorted to work in the Swiss Patent Office in 1901, which didn't stop his brain from running in overdrive. While at the patent office, he completed an astonishing range of theoretical physics publications, written in his spare time, among them, the beginnings of his general theory of relativity. He published his works in final form in 1915, and won the 1921 Nobel Prize for Physics.

Einstein fled Germany in 1933 and was welcomed as professor at Princeton University, where he remained for over 20 years. He was offered, and declined, the second presidency of the state of Israel. He co-founded the Hebrew University of Jerusalem and died peacefully in 1955.

PERSON OF THE CENTURY

TIME

ALBERT EINSTEIN

the handwriting reveals:

- • Somewhat narcissistic and wrapped up in his own needs.
- • Could be inconsiderate and sarcastic.
- • Genius.

robert OPPENHEIMER

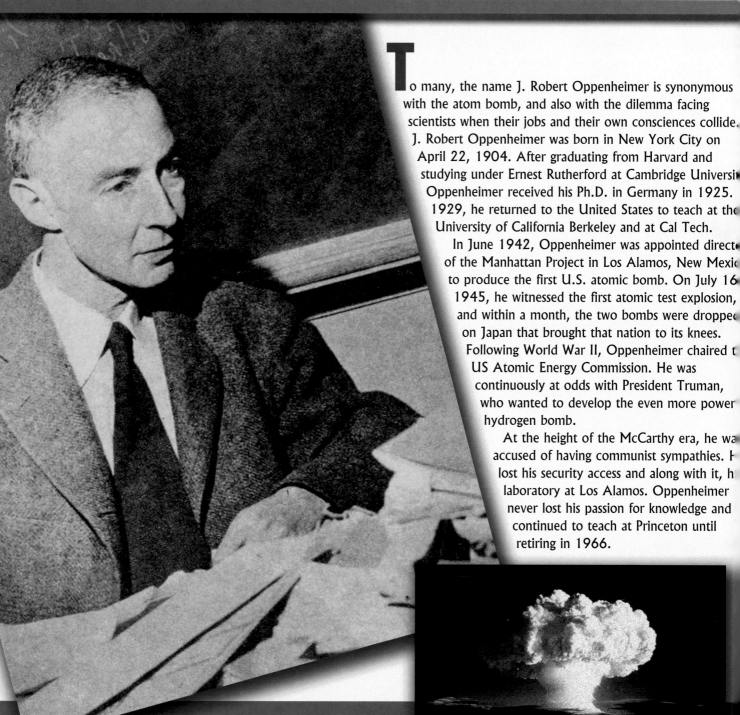

To many, the name J. Robert Oppenheimer is synonymous with the atom bomb, and also with the dilemma facing scientists when their jobs and their own consciences collide. J. Robert Oppenheimer was born in New York City on April 22, 1904. After graduating from Harvard and studying under Ernest Rutherford at Cambridge University, Oppenheimer received his Ph.D. in Germany in 1925. 1929, he returned to the United States to teach at the University of California Berkeley and at Cal Tech.

In June 1942, Oppenheimer was appointed director of the Manhattan Project in Los Alamos, New Mexico to produce the first U.S. atomic bomb. On July 16, 1945, he witnessed the first atomic test explosion, and within a month, the two bombs were dropped on Japan that brought that nation to its knees. Following World War II, Oppenheimer chaired the US Atomic Energy Commission. He was continuously at odds with President Truman, who wanted to develop the even more powerful hydrogen bomb.

At the height of the McCarthy era, he was accused of having communist sympathies. He lost his security access and along with it, his laboratory at Los Alamos. Oppenheimer never lost his passion for knowledge and continued to teach at Princeton until retiring in 1966.

the handwriting reveals:

- A need to compensate for a stormy life by being overly controlling.

- Although outwardly people-oriented, may have had a need to revert to seclusion.

- A genius.

- A reliable and resilient personality, with predictable behavior.

At the height of the McCarthy era, he was accused of having communist sympathies. He lost his security access, and along with it, Los Alamos.

1. Very small handwriting – the combination of high quality and small handwriting indicates a person with a high level of intelligence and great concentrative abilities. He was an excellent conceptual thinker and was attentive to detail.

2. The small handwriting also shows a modest personality with great tenacity and ability to achieve his goals.

3. The large space between his first word and and the next suggests he may have been a cautious person.

4. The large space between the lines indicates a strong need to control the emotional environment and not clutter life with emotional issues.

To Eisenstaedt – for this latest attempt to record men in their most dif- ficult act: thinking greetings –

Robert Oppenheimer

Princeton
November 1947

SLANT: Basically, there are three major directions for the writing:

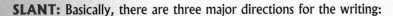

Right slant: Is generally indicative of a more outgoing person. A right slant suggests more extroversion: mental, or actually behavioral. If you want to choose a politician, hire a social worker, sales person or any employee whose position requires good relating skills, you want to select someone who writes with a right slant.

Straight or vertical slant: This is indicative of concentration and those who seek to be in control. Those who write straight up and down usually have their own social agenda and are strong enough to implement it. If the handwriting is very rigid, the writer marches to their own drummer and behaves as if it's "my way or the highway." However, if the handwriting is flexible and looks mature to you, then they are able to be great leaders and listen to the wishes of the people around them.

Left slant: This is an indicator of introversion. Left-slanted writers are people that prefer to stay in their own world. Even if they seem communicative and outgoing, they prefer to keep to themselves and are timid in a crowd. They find it hard at times to intimately connect with others because they don't allow themselves to be immersed in their relationships. Many times they are victims of very strict parents who punished and criticized them in such a way that caused some sort of social phobia to develop.

SIZE: Size of handwriting is determined by the measurement of the height and width of the letter. Usually there are three major sizes:

Small or very small. Small or minute handwriting often suggests introversion and social timidity. Think about the shy boy from your high school who never said a word or had the courage to ask girls out on dates. The size of the handwriting correlates to self-esteem.

Medium size: This writer is generally well adjusted. If the handwriting is "copy book" quality, legible and well punctuated, look for a mainstream all-American guy. He is someone who simply enjoys both worlds; he can be analytical on one hand, yet be warm and emotional on the other. This qualifies him to interact smoothly in social situations.

One of the most valuable usages of graphology is to explore, predict and assess the person's attitude towards the world and his social behavior. The most important clues are the slant of the handwriting, size, margins of the handwriting and legibility.

Large and very large: Large indicates an extroverted personality; a person who wants to show off and be noticed. This is the loudmouth who laughs out loud in a restaurant or the woman who walks on the boardwalk with luxurious, bright clothes.

MARGIN: Margins are the white space around the handwriting. For social relations we look mostly at the right margin. The right side indicates the outside world and relationships to other people. The smaller the right margin, the less considerate the writer is. These people are more likely to be intrusive; but it's a good sign for salespeople who need to have a pushy personality. However, extroverted people, on the whole, usually have a wider right margin.

[Wide margin]   [No margin]

LEGIBILITY: Legibility works in conjunction with other indicators. As a rule of thumb legible handwriting indicates a person who cares about social relations and wants to be understood. Totally messy handwriting (rule out physically ill people) might give us a great clue to a person who is inconsiderate, a serial killer or just a regular sociopath. It can also point to a sever psychological disorder like schizophrenia.

[Legible]

[Illegible]

USING THOSE FOUR ELEMENTS: slant, size, margins and legibility, can give us rich and accurate clues to the likelihood of the kind of social interactions a writer might demonstrate.

He refused to patent his discovery; but in the coming years, his vaccine would virtually eradicate polio.

1. The large space between words indicates a subconscious need to guard his own personal space. He liked doing his thinking by himself.

2. The arched cross bar on the **"t"** suggests a person with a great deal of discipline.

3. The thick, smeared end-stroke indicates the writer has a bit of a temper, perhaps impatience with those who can't keep up.

4. The simplified capital **"S"** is the mark of a cultured person.

5. The large loop in the **"J"** suggests a person who has a strong sensual side.

6. The open **"a"** indicates a talkative nature.

7. The fact that the surname is given equal weight as the first name shows a person comfortable in his own skin, unpretentious and accepting of his family.

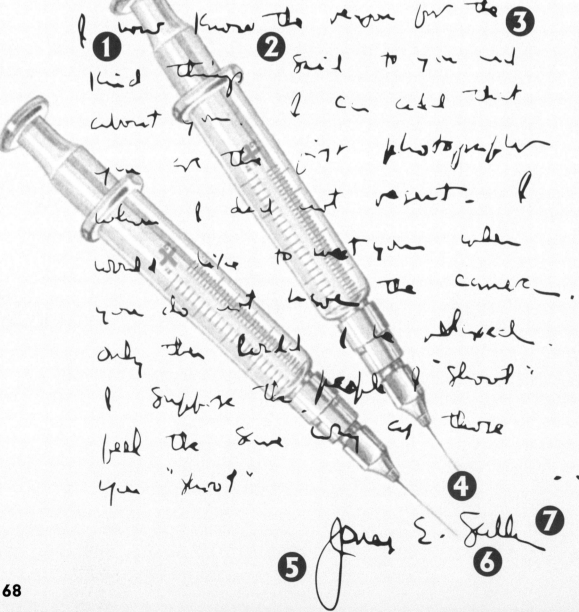

jonas SALK

If Jonas Salk had pursued his original plans, the victory in finding the cure for polio in this country would have happened a lot sooner. Born in 1914 to Russian immigrants in New York City, he was the first member of his family to attend college. He registered at City College intending to study law, but switched his major to medicine and studied influenza at NYU.

The nation was in the throes of a polio epidemic in 1955 – and it was that year that he developed a vaccine at the University of Pittsburgh. He refused to patent his discovery; but in the coming years, his vaccine would virtually eradicate polio.

He founded the Jonas Salk Institute for Biological Studies in La Jolla, California where he intensely worked on a number of scientific causes and disease-related epidemics for over thirty years. He died on June 23, 1995 after spending his final years on a quest to find a cure for AIDS.

the handwriting reveals:

• Complex personality with unpredictabe emotional response.

• A strong ego covered by a warm exterior.

• At times, an unusual approach to the other gender.

• Could be a rigid personality.

benjamin SPOCK

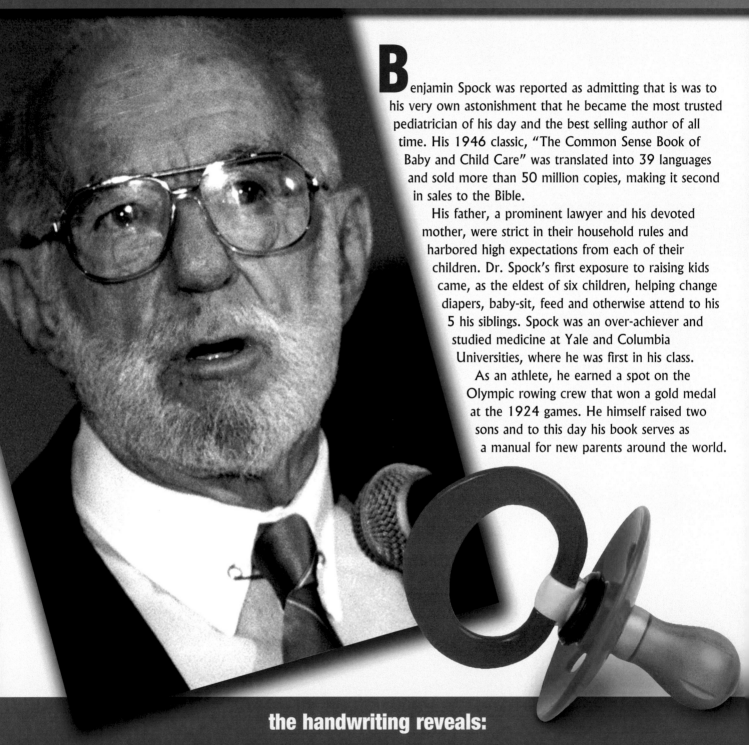

Benjamin Spock was reported as admitting that is was to his very own astonishment that he became the most trusted pediatrician of his day and the best selling author of all time. His 1946 classic, "The Common Sense Book of Baby and Child Care" was translated into 39 languages and sold more than 50 million copies, making it second in sales to the Bible.

His father, a prominent lawyer and his devoted mother, were strict in their household rules and harbored high expectations from each of their children. Dr. Spock's first exposure to raising kids came, as the eldest of six children, helping change diapers, baby-sit, feed and otherwise attend to his 5 his siblings. Spock was an over-achiever and studied medicine at Yale and Columbia Universities, where he was first in his class. As an athlete, he earned a spot on the Olympic rowing crew that won a gold medal at the 1924 games. He himself raised two sons and to this day his book serves as a manual for new parents around the world.

the handwriting reveals:

- Witty, with a strong sense of humor.

- A curious mind, with a need to explore everything around him.

- A subconsciously strong need to command people.

- A creative personality.

His classic on child raising sold more than 50 million copies – second only to the Bible.

1. The **"B"** is open at the base, denoting a very talkative and verbal personality.

2. The **"B"** is sharply pointed at the top: a strong, analytical person who will fight for his beliefs.

3. The **"n"** is very angular indicating an analytical mind

4. The **"S"** is simplified: good taste and a cultured personality with a no-nonsense approach to problem-solving.

5. The **"p"** is open and broken in two parts signifying a very energetic person who needs to connect with the future. The pointed part in the lower zone might indicate some aggressive tendencies toward others.

6. The **"k"** is pointed suggesting an aggressive personality and again a no-nonsense approach to life.

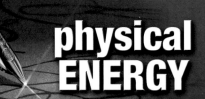

physical ENERGY

A long and heavy "t" cross bar is one of the most important indicators of energy: This person is going to go the whole nine yards. He or she will work a 16-hour day.

Heavy-looking writing: Many serial killers and people who do heavy physical labor write this way. It represents the displacement of mental energy into the physical world rather than into the philosophical world.

Listless writing: The non crossing "t" bar indicates a person who has no energy, or is weak and depressed. The writer has subconscious feelings of helplessness when trying to tackle challenges in his world.

Short lower zone: A person who prefers the intellectual versus physical expression. This writer learned from a young age that he can escape to daydreaming and fantasy rather than deal with the real world.

Weak "t" cross bars: This is a sure sign of someone who has difficulties finishing what he starts. He is mentally tied up with unresolved personal issues which take their toll on his real world achievements. This person is very likely an underachiever.

Angular handwriting: This is usually indicative of a person who is very dynamic, physically strong and active. This writer doesn't like to cut corners when it comes to being direct and efficient.

Club-like ending of lower zone: This indicates a physical energy that could be used sadistically and violently. Joseph Stalin, the Russian dictator who killed thousands and thousands of his countryman, had this kind of club-like ending in his handwriting.

sports

howard COSELL

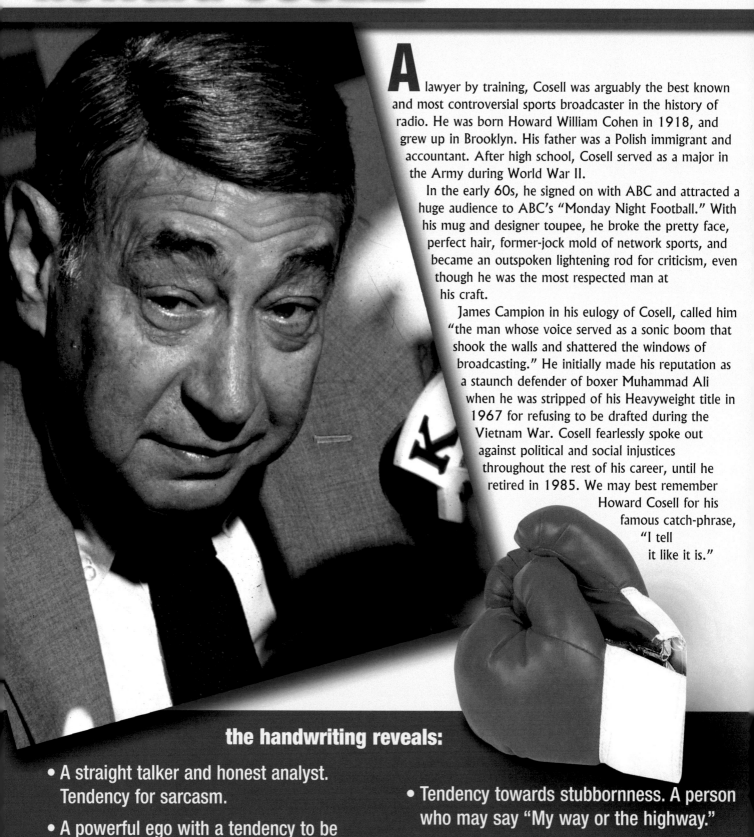

A lawyer by training, Cosell was arguably the best known and most controversial sports broadcaster in the history of radio. He was born Howard William Cohen in 1918, and grew up in Brooklyn. His father was a Polish immigrant and accountant. After high school, Cosell served as a major in the Army during World War II.

In the early 60s, he signed on with ABC and attracted a huge audience to ABC's "Monday Night Football." With his mug and designer toupee, he broke the pretty face, perfect hair, former-jock mold of network sports, and became an outspoken lightening rod for criticism, even though he was the most respected man at his craft.

James Campion in his eulogy of Cosell, called him "the man whose voice served as a sonic boom that shook the walls and shattered the windows of broadcasting." He initially made his reputation as a staunch defender of boxer Muhammad Ali when he was stripped of his Heavyweight title in 1967 for refusing to be drafted during the Vietnam War. Cosell fearlessly spoke out against political and social injustices throughout the rest of his career, until he retired in 1985. We may best remember Howard Cosell for his famous catch-phrase, "I tell it like it is."

the handwriting reveals:

- A straight talker and honest analyst. Tendency for sarcasm.

- A powerful ego with a tendency to be opinionated and have a combustible nature.

- Tendency towards stubbornness. A person who may say "My way or the highway."

- Intellectual capacity to dissect every event into tiny component parts.

> "There was no crusade too big, no injustice too imposing, and no human power too intimidating for his prodding sarcasm and razor-sharp wit." – James Campion

1. The **"H"** shows an additional stroke before the cross bar: a sensitive personality that hated interference.

2. The **"e"** looks like a Greek letter signifying he had aesthetic values.

3. The **"d"** has a high, full loop, indicating a sensitive and creative imagination.

4. The **"y"** has a heavy, straight end stroke, suggesting a stubborn personality.

5. The signature is underlined: a strong, secure personality.

6. The **"ll"** sports no loops implying honesty but also a tendency towards sarcasm.

Spitz' exploits in Munich elevated him to the rank of one of the greatest competitive swimmers of all time.

1. The beginning stroke is very long: In business deals, this person likes to think before he reacts.

2. The **"S"** leans backward suggesting a tendency not to reveal one's true self.

3. The **"S"** also has a small, locked loop, indicating a critical personality.

4. The **"i"** dot stands just behind the stem. This is associated with a tendency for procrastination.

5. The **"t"** cross bar is short, indicating a somewhat conventional personality.

6. The **"t"** cross bar goes through the middle of the stem signifying a cautious and responsible personality. This person has a great deal on his mind.

mark SPITZ

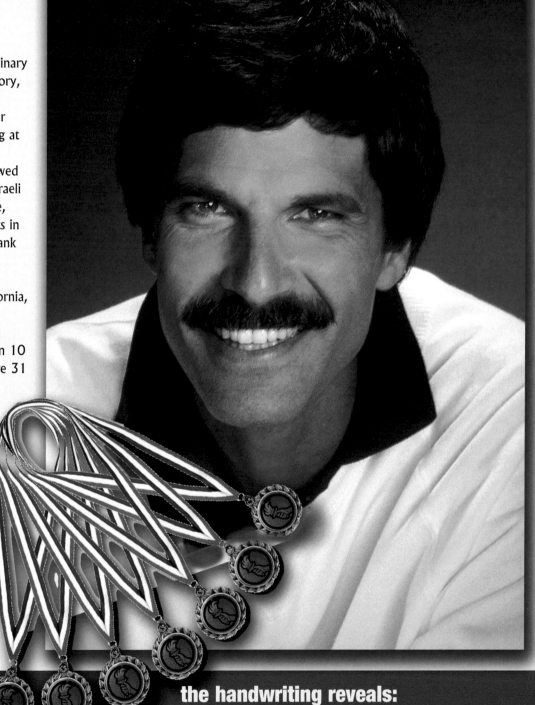

In one of the most extraordinary performances in Olympic history, Mark Spitz won a remarkable seven gold medals and set four individual records in swimming at the 1972 Olympic games in Munich. Although overshadowed by the tragic murder of 11 Israeli athletes in the Olympic village, Spitz's unworldly achievements in Munich elevated him to the rank of the greatest competitive swimmer of all time.

A native of Modesto, California, Spitz began his career by participating in the Maccabiah games in 1965, where he won 10 medals. He went on to capture 31 National Amateur Athletic Union titles, eight NCAA championships and five Pan American gold medals, setting 333 world records in the process. Additionally, he won two gold medals in relay events at the 1968 Games in Mexico City.

- Hard on himself.

- He has a strong sense of humility, but is a no- nonsense kind of guy.

the handwriting reveals:

- A strong intellect.

- Extremely highly driven, motivated, and competitive.

sandy KOUFAX

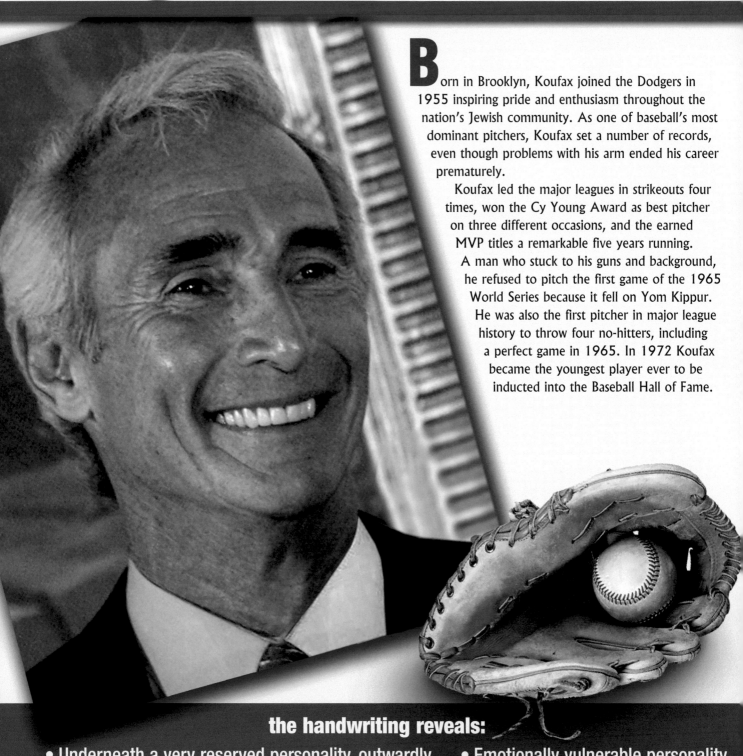

Born in Brooklyn, Koufax joined the Dodgers in 1955 inspiring pride and enthusiasm throughout the nation's Jewish community. As one of baseball's most dominant pitchers, Koufax set a number of records, even though problems with his arm ended his career prematurely.

Koufax led the major leagues in strikeouts four times, won the Cy Young Award as best pitcher on three different occasions, and the earned MVP titles a remarkable five years running. A man who stuck to his guns and background, he refused to pitch the first game of the 1965 World Series because it fell on Yom Kippur. He was also the first pitcher in major league history to throw four no-hitters, including a perfect game in 1965. In 1972 Koufax became the youngest player ever to be inducted into the Baseball Hall of Fame.

the handwriting reveals:

- Underneath a very reserved personality, outwardly shy and humble, lies a vibrant, strong mind that is constantly active and absorbing the environment.

- A very strong intellectual personality with strong love of reading, which helps him escape.

- Emotionally vulnerable personality who is able to hide the extent of his hurt.

- Strong preoccupation with physical pleasures.

He refused to pitch the first game of the 1965 World Series; it fell on Yom Kippur.

1. The **"n"** looks like a thread, indicating diplomatic skills and avoidance of confrontation.

2. The **"S"** upper loop is full indicating a mind that works overtime and absorbs information like a sponge.

3. The **"d"** has a full stem, meaning the writer can be very emotional and sensitive.

4. The **"K"** is divided into two, indicating that the writer is an individualist, and can be nonconformist: he doesn't always go along with the crowd.

5. The **"f"** has a narrow upper loop, suggesting he is not always able to connect openly with his emotions.

6. The upper part of the **"x"** is closed and elongated, suggesting an intellectual mind that loves to read.

7. The **"f"** has a full-blown lower zone: a practical, self-reliant personality with the ability to enjoy good food.

8. The **"y"** has a short stem meaning a very agile mind.

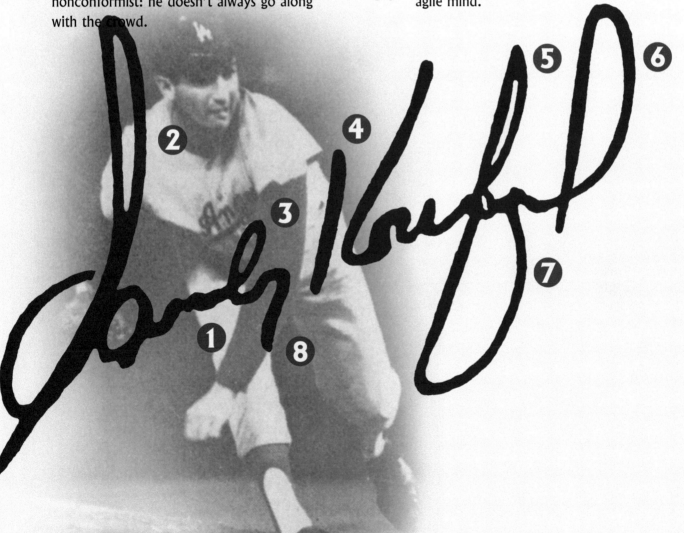

Jews & the Olympics
'72 Munich Games

The blackest moment in Olympic history took place in 1972 with a terrorist attack on Israeli athletes. But before we delve into what happened there, let's look at the Jewish legacy in the world of sports.

Throughout history, the Jews have been better known for their intellectual and financial abilities rather then their athleticism, although according to Judaism, a "healthy mind in healthy body" is a must. But there is a proud legacy of Jewish athletes:

- Can you name a Jewish Olympic gymnast who won 10 medals in three Olympiads during the 1940s and 1950s? **Agnes Keleti.**

- Can you name a Jewish southpaw who hurled two no-hitters but who never pitched for the Dodgers? **Ken Holtzman.**

- Did you know that one of Spain's most celebrated bullfighters, lavishly praised by Ernest Hemingway, was a Jewish boy from Brooklyn? **It was Sidney Franklin.**

- What Olympic swimmer from Hungary broke 10 world records, five Olympic records, and an amazing 107 Hungarian National records? **Eva Szekely.**

Arnold "Red" Auerbach worked as coach and general manager of the Boston Celtics and became a legend in his own time. His team won nine National Basketball Association titles (eight in a row) from 1959-1966. **Mark Spitz** won seven gold medals in the Munich Olympic Games in 1972, breaking all records.

However his winning streak came into stark contrast with one of the darkest moments in modern Jewish and modern sports history.

It was 4:30 in the morning on Sept. 5, 1972, when five Arab terrorists wearing track sweat-suits climbed the six-foot six-inch fence surrounding the Olympic Village in Munich. These five were met by three more men who are presumed to have obtained credentials to enter the village.

Just before 5:00 a.m., the Arabs knocked on the door of Israeli wrestling Coach Moshe Weinberg. When Weinberg opened the door he realized something was wrong and shouted a warning to his comrades. He and weightlifter Joseph Romano attempted to block the door while other Israelis escaped, but the terrorists killed them. The Arabs then succeeded in rounding up nine Israelis to hold as hostages.

At 9:30, the terrorists announced that they were Palestinians and demanded that Israel release 200 Arab prisoners and that the terrorists be given safe passage out of Germany.

After hours of tense negotiations, the Palestinians, who it was later learned belonged to a PLO faction called "Black September," agreed to a plan whereby they were to be taken by helicopter to the NATO air base at Firstenfeldbruck where they would be given an airplane to fly them and their hostages to Cairo. The Israelis were then taken by bus to the helicopters and flown to the airfield. In the course of the transfer, the Germans discovered that there were eight terrorists instead of the five they expected and realized that they had not assigned enough marksmen to carry out the plan to kill the terrorists at the airport.

After the helicopters landed at the air base around 10:30 p.m., the German sharpshooters attempted to kill the terrorists and a bloody firefight ensued... a terrorist grenade blew up one of the helicopters holding the Israelis. The remaining hostages in the second helicopter

Munich1972

were shot to death by one of the surviving terrorists.

At 3 a.m., a drawn and teary-eyed Jim McKay, who had been reporting the drama throughout the day as part of ABC's Olympic coverage, announced: "They're all gone."

Five of the terrorists were killed along with one policeman, and three were captured. A little over a month later, on Oct. 29, terrorists demanding that the Munich killers be released hijacked a Lufthansa jet.

The Germans capitulated and the terrorists were let go, but an Israeli assassination squad was assigned to track them down along with those responsible for planning the massacre...

Meanwhile, the mastermind of the massacre remains at large. In fact, in 1999, Abu Daoud admitted his role in his autobiography, "Memoirs of a Palestinian Terrorist." He claims his commandos never intended to harm the athletes and blamed their deaths on the German police and the stubbornness of then-Israeli Prime Minister Golda Meir

The massacre of 11 Israeli athletes was not considered sufficiently serious to merit canceling or postponing the Olympics. "Incredibly, they're going on with it," Jim Murray of the Los Angeles Times wrote at the time. "It's almost like having a dance at Dachau."

"Be strong and courageous. Do not be afraid or terrified because of them, for the Lord your God goes with you; he will never leave you nor forsake you."

Deuteronomy 31:6

The Israeli Olympic team parades in the Olympic Stadium, Munich, Aug. 26, 1972 during the opening ceremony of the 1972 Olympic Games. Joseph Inbar, the father of our visual director Gadi Inbar, is pictured fifth from the right.

another career

Jerry Seinfeld:
PHILOSOPHER

Look at the **"i"** and the **"d."** The **"i"** dot and stem of the **"d"** are very tall; the **"d"** loop is high and full. Seinfeld likes to think and process information. He also absorbs the world around him and tries to get to the bottom of it all.

Bette Midler:
MOTIVATIONAL SPEAKER

Look at the **"t"** cross bar. It is very strong and powerful. She likes to push people ahead. The **"d"** shows us a very sensitive and creative person who can listen and emote with the audience. The ending **"r"** indicates that Midler is both diplomatic and a person who won't let others push her around.

Sandy Koufax:
LITERARY CRITIC

Look at the small handwriting which indicates a very analytical mind with an attention for details. The long **"S"** and the final **"x"** indicate a literary ability, a sensitivity for the written word.

Gloria Steinem:
CIA OPERATIVE/INTERROGATOR

You can see how the handwriting is vertical and left, meaning she cannot let herself get engulfed with the clients. She has a probing, analytical mind and a good memory. That qualifies her to analyze the answers of prisoners of war. She is relentless as you can see by the angular handwriting which means that she can wear the detainees down. The **"t"** cross bar indicates her tenacity and relentlessness, like a Pit-Bull dog who has his prey in his claws and won't let go.

musicians & artists

leonard BERNSTEIN

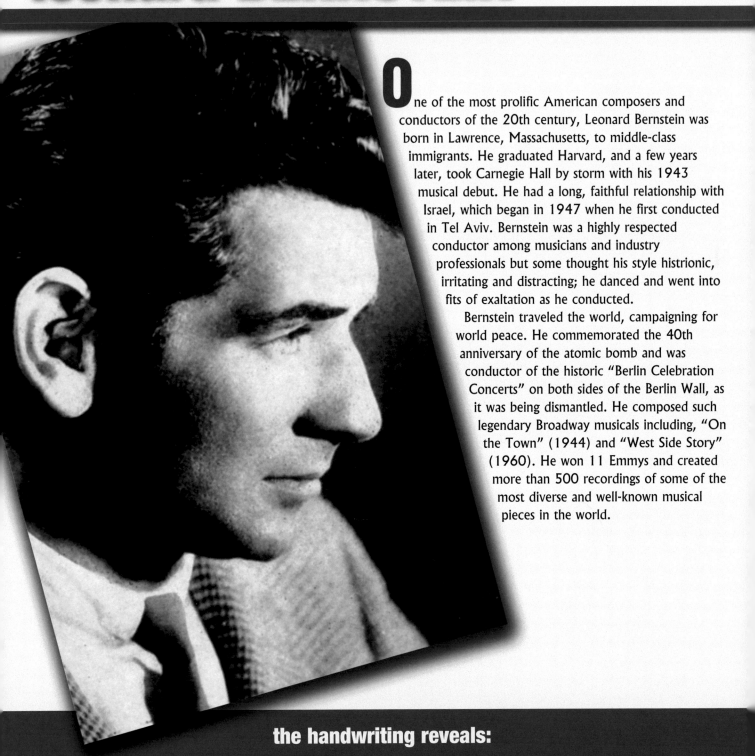

One of the most prolific American composers and conductors of the 20th century, Leonard Bernstein was born in Lawrence, Massachusetts, to middle-class immigrants. He graduated Harvard, and a few years later, took Carnegie Hall by storm with his 1943 musical debut. He had a long, faithful relationship with Israel, which began in 1947 when he first conducted in Tel Aviv. Bernstein was a highly respected conductor among musicians and industry professionals but some thought his style histrionic, irritating and distracting; he danced and went into fits of exaltation as he conducted.

Bernstein traveled the world, campaigning for world peace. He commemorated the 40th anniversary of the atomic bomb and was conductor of the historic "Berlin Celebration Concerts" on both sides of the Berlin Wall, as it was being dismantled. He composed such legendary Broadway musicals including, "On the Town" (1944) and "West Side Story" (1960). He won 11 Emmys and created more than 500 recordings of some of the most diverse and well-known musical pieces in the world.

the handwriting reveals:

- He did not learn this handwriting in school; he had an extremely colorful imagination.

- He marched in tune to his own drummer, incorporating his ambition into his life.

- He had limitless energy, but at the same time displayed stubbornness.

- The writer had a flair for artistic and unconventional behavior.

Some thought his style histrionic, irritating and distracting; he danced and went into fits of exultation as he conducted.

1. The hook and rounded **"F"** suggests a person with great tenacity.

2. The Greek-style **"E"** indicates a love of culture.

3. The lopsided final **"t"** shows a writer who is unafraid to use pressure to attain his goals.

4. The small **"a"** ending with a down stroke under the baseline shows a person with strong likes and dislikes.

5. The incredibly simple **"p"** suggests a quick-thinking, goal-oriented mind.

6. The **"L"** with the hook at the top indicates a person with jealousy issues.

7. The large belly on the **"B"** is typical of a writer who is attuned to his tactile sense.

The Divine Miss M sang her hit from "Beaches" – "Wind Beneath My Wings" to Johnny Carson on his last night on television.

1. The **"B"** is open at the bottom indicating a very talkative personality.

2. The lower zone of the **"f"** is full meaning a tendency to be strong, down-to-earth, practical, and in touch with her feelings.

3. The **"y"** is straight and hooked suggesting a strong mind with a need to get to the bottom of things.

4. The **"r"** has an extremely long end stroke – indicating a strong tendency to achieve one's goals.

5. The **"M"** is looped indicating a highly emotional and driven personality.

6. The **"t"** cross is very long – typical of a motivated, goal-driven, take charge personality who can bring projects to their completion.

7. The **"B"** is looped – suggesting a tendency towards self-absorption.

bette MIDLER

"T he Divine Miss M" was destined for the stage at birth, after all her parents named her after Bette Davis. She honed in on her performance skills as early as elementary school in her native Hawaii, where she was the only Jewish girl. She learned to make her classmates laugh to escape ridicule.

Midler got her first TV role while studying drama in college, the catalyst to her move to New York City in 1965. Her voice and outrageous talent landed her some of the best Broadway roles, after which she developed a nightclub act for the gay bath houses which were perfect for her brand of bawdiness. That period established a following among gay men, whose loyalty has endured throughout her career.

She began the 1970s with complete recognition from the music industry, winning Grammy awards for more than one album, which eventually took her to Hollywood and launched her film career. Her first film, "The Rose," won Midler an Oscar nomination and two Golden Globe awards. Since then, her path has been strewn with successful albums, movies, tours and plays, earning her the indisputable title of Diva, a.k.a., "The Divine Miss M."

the handwriting reveals:

- Extremely strong, powerful personality.

- High-strung, vibrant, energetic, driven.

- She engulfs people with her energy, enthusiasm, and infectious personality.

- Her ego can easily get hurt and she reacts to that in her own way.

aaron COPLAND

For the better part of four decades, Aaron Copland was considered "The Leader" of American composers. Copland learned piano from an older sister and by the time he reached 15 he had made up his mind that all he wanted to do was to write music. In 1921, he studied in Paris and began composing classical works with jazz infusion. His series of hit ballets, choreographed by the legendary Martha Graham, include: "Billy the Kid," "Rodeo" and "Appalachian Spring," and began gaining national momentum in the late 1930s. At the onset of World War II, Copland had risen to the top of his craft. During the war, he produced "A Lincoln Portrait" and later "Fanfare for the Common Man," earning him international acclaim.

After the war, the Schoenberg School of Atonal Music took hold and the effect on him, writes friend Leonard Bernstein, was "heartbreaking." His composing tapered off sharply, but he wrote some memorable film scores and continued writing, lecturing, teaching and receiving an outpouring of honors throughout his remaining years.

the handwriting reveals:

- The writer at times had a very spiritual personality. In addition he was constantly aspiring to new and higher goals.

- Someone who could often be aggressive.

- A very direct, simple and secure person who did not need to show off.

- Curious: needed to know what was going on around him at all times.

1. The **"A"** is open to the right, indicating a great deal of emotional honesty.

2. The **"r"** is pointed, showing a very perceptive and probing mind. He could take things as they were, but had to get to the bottom of them.

3. The **"p"** looks like a cane, showing artistic and musical ability.

4. The **"I"** stands tall and has a full loop, suggesting pride and idealism – a very sensitive and emotional nature.

5. The **"n"** looks like the letter "u" – Copland was a charmer and friendly; he knew how to find his way into people's hearts.

Caricature by Antonio Sotomayor.

> "During the first decades of the 20th century, Chagall created a personal mythology; bringing poetry back into painting… his was an art of poetic irrationality and private memories." – Acquavella Galleries

1. The **"M"** is very tall with sharp humps indicating a spiritually inquisitive and strong penetrating mind, impatient at times.

2. Space between the letters suggests a highly intuitive personality which let him disengage from pure logical thinking.

3. The **"a"** is open at the top, typical of a talkative personality with much sincerity and need for fresh air.

4. The **"I"** has a very long and stretched end stroke, indicating a need for personal space.

5. Underlined signature shows a subconscious need to feel secure.

marc CHAGALL

Mark Zakharovich Shagal was born in 1887 in Belarus, and began sketching during his youth. In his early 20's Chagall lived in several of the cultural capitals of Europe, including St. Petersburg, Paris and Berlin, where he found patrons, befriended a dozen famous artists, and opened his first studios. In 1915, he returned to his native Belarus and thrived under the new Communist regime until he was deemed a political exile by the government in 1923.

He returned to France, where he settled until 1941 and launched one of his most prolific artistic periods. When the Nazis took over France, he found refuge in New York, designing scenery and costumes for the stage, and grasping any opportunity to exhibit his works in New York and Paris.

After the war, he returned to France where he lived for the rest of his life. Despite some dark moments is his personal life, he remained an optimist. With every brushstroke, every green, blue, or purple face of his violinists, every kiss and every embrace of his lovers, his creativity was fueled in monumental proportions. In his last years he had the privilege to witness his own fame, being regarded as one of the world's leading artists.

the handwriting reveals:

- Childlike personality.

- Built and lived in his own imaginative world.

- Vivid and creative imagination.

- Strong, flamboyant interaction with the world around him.

irving BERLIN

Irving Berlin is one of the great American success stories. As a child of poverty, young Berlin took any odd job to support his family which gave him the drive to achieve his destiny as one the world's great songwriters. He wrote such memorable pieces as "God Bless America" and "White Christmas," that have become staples of American culture. He grew up on the streets of New York and started composing songs at 19. In World War I he joined the Army and directed the group band, "Yip Yip Yaphank." In 1933, he produced original scores for Fred Astaire, for whom he wrote "White Christmas" for the 1942 film "Holiday Inn." His biggest hits came after World War II with "Annie Get Your Gun," starring the legendary Ethel Merman, and "Call me Madam" in 1950. After the success of "Miss Liberty" and "Mr. President" (1962), Berlin lost his passion for the limelight and led a more humble and solitary lifestyle, making occasional public appearances, receiving numerous awards, medals, and honors. Upon his death, Berlin had left behind a stunning legacy of over 1,200 songs, including some of the most performed musical pieces in American popular music.

the handwriting reveals:

- A personality with a great deal of intuition and thinking out of the box.

- May have liked to be in control as a way to keep up defenses against inner demons.

- May not always have been the easiest person to live with. Possibly irritable and argumentative.

- Tendency for insecurity and self doubts.

A poor boy selling newspapers grows up to write "God Bless America."

1. The **"n"** end stroke is clubbed, indicating a tendency to be opinionated; not always diplomatic.

2. The **"g"** is hooked signifying nervousness and some difficulties consummating matrimonial relations.

3. The **"st"** is smeared indicating a great deal of anxiety with emotional difficulties.

4. The **"t"** cross bar is traced, suggesting a strong and tenacious personality.

5. The **"l"** is looped implying a strong influence by his father.

6. The **"i"** is very high and dashed denoting a wonderful imagination with a vivid mind.

THEATRE arts
complete text "THE LEADING LADY" by Ruth Gordon
FEBRUARY 1950
50¢

IRVING BERLIN

I hope you get a good one - If not dont blame me - I did everything you said. - many thanks and best wishes

Irving Berlin

The Jewish Hungarian conductor who dared to conduct the Nazi hero Richard Wagner.

1. The **"G"** looks like a musical note with a straight down stroke; this indicates he subconsciously identified himself with his profession. Had an agile, penetrating, no-nonsense mind.

2. The **"g"** lower loop is very low and small, suggesting that he may have experienced some disappointments in his relationships.

3. The **"S"** is simple, angular at the bottom and hooked – The writer had highly cultured taste with a mind that did not let go. Tendency for decisiveness and tough attitude.

4. The **"t"** stem is very looped – meaning an extremely sensitive personality, associated with great creativity and at the same time real vulnerability to criticism.

george SOLTI

George Stein, more commonly known as George Solti, was born in 1912 in Budapest, Hungary. He studied piano and composition with Zoltan Kodaly and Bela Bartok, giving his first concert at the age of twelve. Solti began working as assistant at the Budapest Opera in 1930 and was Director of Music there from 1934 to 1939.

After the outbreak of the Second World War, Solti immigrated to Zurich, and resumed his career as a pianist. He won first prize at the Geneva International Competition in 1942. For almost 25 years, he concentrated entirely on conducting operas. In the late 1950's he had moved to America and by 1961 was appointed Musical Director of the Los Angeles Philharmonic Orchestra, and his assistant was none other than Zubin Mehta.

In 1969 he took over as director of the Chicago Symphony Orchestra, where his second career as an orchestra conductor began and where he held his post until 1991. During his time conducting the Chicago Symphony Orchestra, he was also director of the Orchestre de Paris. George Solti died on September 5, 1997 in Antibes, France.

the handwriting reveals:

- A very powerful, dynamic personality.

- In touch with the physical side of his nature.

- Unique and unorthodox personality.

- Work-oriented and exuberant; able to motivate others to work.

Gallery of Jewish Musicians & Radio/Media Personalities

The Jews, as we discussed, had a significant part in creating a global empire out of "Hollywood," and the film, television and radio industries (with enthusiastic influences in comedy, music and theatre as well) from the very beginning.

For Jews, humor is just as significant a part of the culture as it is of a religious existence. The fact that the number of Jewish comics is so disproportionate to their percentage of the population proves the profound link between Jews and humor. Why is that?

Freud had two explanations:
- One is that comedy and jokes are a kind of masked aggression. It is easier to get even with someone with a punch-line than to punch them in the nose. The Jews, after all, are "People of The Book."

- The second interpretation is that humor is sublimation, a way to deal with anxiety. When you laugh, you abolish stress. Here is a short list of comedians:

- **Woody Allen** portrays the intellectual neurotic observer.

- **Jack Benny,** the master of timing.

- **Groucho Marx'** wit was at a Talmudic (highly evolved) level.

- **Milton Berle** memorized thousands of jokes and was the first variety show on television. Restaurants and bars had to close because their patrons were staying at home to watch him.

- **Jackie Mason** uses his profound insight into the Jewish character to fire up his comedy.

- **Mel Brooks** goes so far as to invent American Indians who spoke Yiddish.

- **George Burns** played God, and lived to 101.

- **Jerry Seinfeld's** show ran away with the highest sitcom ratings.

Plus, Jewish talent spread to the more sophisticated media of television. Here is a short list of media personalities:

- **Barbara Walters** is another star of the media; she became the co-host of the "Today Show" in 1974. She pulled off a string of exclusive interviews with personalities of international status, such as Fidel Castro and Anwar Sadat.

- **Mike Wallace** helped make "60 Minutes" the most popular news magazine program on the air.

- **Larry King** ranks as the king of interviews. He was raised in a kosher home in Brooklyn. His show reaches seven million people in the United States alone.

Jewish talent spread from the Yiddish Theatre to Broadway:

- **Arthur Hammerstein** produced countless musicals on Broadway from the teens through the 1930s.

- **Richard Rodgers and Oscar Hammerstein** together wrote "Oklahoma," "Carousel," "South Pacific," and "Annie Get Your Gun."

- **Frank Loesser** wrote the music and lyrics for "Guys and Dolls," "Ain't Misbehavin," "The Most Happy Fella," and "How to Succeed in Business Without Really Trying."

- **Alan Lerner and Frederick Loewe** wrote "My Fair Lady," "Paint Your Wagon," "Brigadoon," and "Camelot."

- **Leonard Bernstein** wrote the music for "West Side Story," "Wonderful Town," "Candide," and several other works on Broadway.

- Playwright **Lillian Hellmann** saw "The Children's Hour," "Little Foxes," "Another Part of the Forest," plus a half-dozen other plays produced on Broadway.

- **Arthur Miller** wrote the classics "Death of a Salesman," "The Crucible," "After the Fall," plus "A View from the Bridge."

- **Sheldon Harnick and Jerry Bach**, lyricist and songwriter, wrote "Fiddler on the Roof," "The Apple Tree," "The Rothschilds," and "Fiorello" together.

- **Barbara Streisand** starred on Broadway in "Funny Girl," and "I Can Get It for You Wholesale."

- **Irwin Shaw** wrote serious drama: "Bury the Dead," "Siege," "The Assassin," and "The Gentle People."

- **Brothers George and Ira Gershwin** wrote over two dozen Broadway musicals, and revolutionized the genre. "Porgy and Bess" was the first musical to win the Pulitzer Prize for Drama.

- **Serge Koussevitzky** conducted the Boston Symphony Orchestra.

- **Bruno Walter** led the New York Philharmonic.

- **Vladimir Horowitz and Arthur Rubinstein** were arguably the greatest pianists in the modern era.

- **Isaac Stern**, the internationally famous virtuoso violinist, has been called America's greatest musical ambassador.

- **Violinists Isaac Perleman, Yehudi Menuhin, Jascha Heifetz and Mischa Elman** – all are in a league of their own.

- **Benny Goodman**, the son of an immigrant tailor from Warsaw, became an icon of the Big Band Era of the 1930s and 40s. Goodman was the first major white bandleader who employed black and white musicians together on stage.

"Praise the Lord with the harp; make music to him on the ten-stringed lyre. Sing to him a new song; play skillfully, and shout for joy."

Psalm 33:2-3

billy JOEL

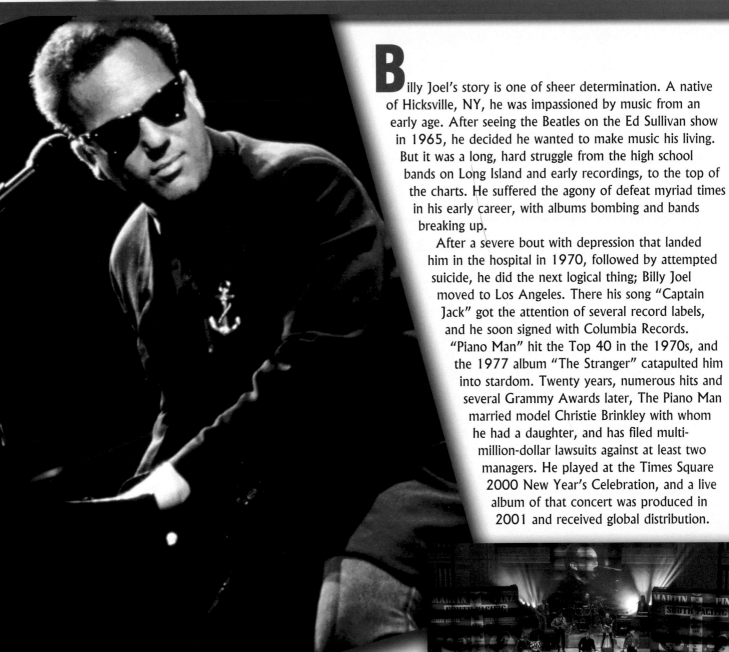

Billy Joel's story is one of sheer determination. A native of Hicksville, NY, he was impassioned by music from an early age. After seeing the Beatles on the Ed Sullivan show in 1965, he decided he wanted to make music his living. But it was a long, hard struggle from the high school bands on Long Island and early recordings, to the top of the charts. He suffered the agony of defeat myriad times in his early career, with albums bombing and bands breaking up.

After a severe bout with depression that landed him in the hospital in 1970, followed by attempted suicide, he did the next logical thing; Billy Joel moved to Los Angeles. There his song "Captain Jack" got the attention of several record labels, and he soon signed with Columbia Records. "Piano Man" hit the Top 40 in the 1970s, and the 1977 album "The Stranger" catapulted him into stardom. Twenty years, numerous hits and several Grammy Awards later, The Piano Man married model Christie Brinkley with whom he had a daughter, and has filed multi-million-dollar lawsuits against at least two managers. He played at the Times Square 2000 New Year's Celebration, and a live album of that concert was produced in 2001 and received global distribution.

the handwriting reveals:

- Holds extremely high aspirations in every endeavor.

- Late adolescence: young at heart.

- Outgoing, extroverted and able to carry out his ideas.

- Needs to control and direct other people's activities.

He suffered the agony of defeat early in his career, with albums bombing and bands disbanding.

1. The **"B"** is open at the bottom: associated with a great deal of desire for self knowledge.

2. The **"i"** dot stands very high and slants backward, showing spiritual awareness with hesitation in performing mundane tasks.

3. The capital **"J"** is concave, suggesting a need to be the center of attention.

4. The **"o"** has a loop, indicating an artist with some tendencies for secretiveness.

5. The lower stem of the **"y"** is short, which may indicate aggressiveness and strong decisiveness.

His name is virtually synonymous with Jewish and Israeli music and songs.

1. The **"Y"** is concave: may sometimes exhibit unreasonable behavior.

2. The **"j"** lower loop shows musical abilities along with intense sexuality.

3. The **"i"** dot slanted to the right suggests that at times he can be very impatient and short-tempered if things don't go his way.

4. The simplistic **"r"** signifies a quick, active mind.

5. Signature: The signature is unique. It indicates a person who is very dynamic, future-oriented and who can think outside the box. One expects him to toss aside social norms that seem to him confining or unjustified.

theodore BIKEL

Born in Vienna, Austria, which he fled at 14 after the Nazi occupation, Theodore Bikel spent the rest of adolescence in Palestine and began his acting career at the Hebrew National Theater. At 22 he moved to London to further his acting studies and make his stage debut. He made his first film debut as a German soldier in "The African Queen" (1951).

After working on "The African Queen," Bikel immigrated to the United States, and obtained more than 100 major dramatic roles on American television. He also appeared on Broadway as Captain George Von Trapp in "The Sound of Music," and in 1969 as Tevye in "Fiddler on the Roof."

His second love was folk music; in fact, his name is virtually synonymous with Jewish and Israeli music and songs.

Bikel delved into politics with the American Jewish Congress, serving as a delegate to the Democratic National Convention in 1968, and protested against Apartheid in front of the South African Embassy in Washington D.C., where he was arrested in 1984. He co-founded the Newport Folk Festival and was appointed by President Carter to the National Council for the Arts.

the handwriting reveals:

- A very unusual non-conforming personality.

- Marched to his own inner drummer.

- Extremely intuitive, creative personality with a restless, high-strung inner self.

- Addicted to the limelight – he will never end up at a monastery in Tibet.

Nobel Prize Winners

The question has always asked again and again: what drives the Jews to achieve intellectual notoriety? One of the ways to try to answer this question is to look at the gallery of Nobel Prize winners. The Jews comprise less than one quarter of one percent of the world's population; but 21 percent of Nobel Prize winners have been Jews. Plus, it is safe to say that the three most influential thinkers of our modern history were Karl Marx, Sigmund Freud, and Albert Einstein.

The question remains: Why do Jews excel in intellectual fields? Here are some possible explanations:

1. In early Christianity, if someone was bright, often he or she would join the church, become celibate and dedicate his or her life to God. Thus, many lines of superior genetic excellence were wiped out.

2. If a Jewish man was brilliant, he got married early to a rich woman who could support him. They had several children who got better medical care; they lived longer and through the generations the genetics created more and more brilliant Jews.

3. Another explanation is that Jews were the most persecuted people. They did not have it easy. In order to survive they had to sharpen their wits to learn how to be more crafty and street-smart.

4. The most important variable is, of course, the Jewish value system. Reading and studying is probably considered one of the most admired and mandatory of pursuits. Since Jews were forbidden from worshiping statues and idols like the other nations, they had to emphasize the written word. Three-year-olds were taught to read.

Among the famous Nobel Prize winners are **physicists** like Albert Einstein, Niels Boher, Enrico Fermi, Rabi Isidor Issac; **writers** like Isaac Bashevis Singer, Elie Wiesel, Boris Pasternak, Shai Agnon ,and Nelly Sacks; **politicians** Henry Kissinger and Menachem Begin; **economists** Paul Anthony Samuelson, Milton Friedman, Herbert A. Simon and Daniel Kahneman.

"Blessed is the man who finds wisdom, the man who gains understanding, for she is more profitable than silver and yields better returns than gold."

Proverbs: 3:13-14

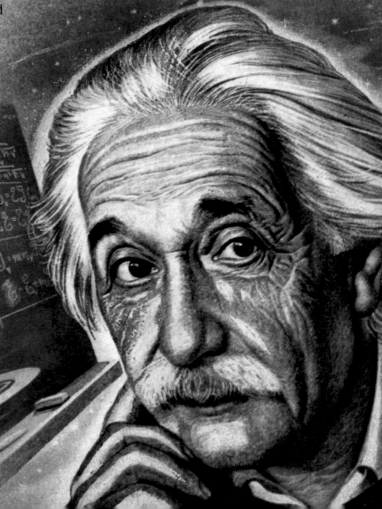

philosophers
spiritual leaders

The Jewish doctor who revealed the subconscious and who popularized cocaine at the turn of the century.

1. The sharp right-ward slant of his writing indicates an energetic, relentless personality.

2. The jagged-edged **"m"** suggests a very sharp, analytical, possibly sarcastic personality.

3. The whiplash end stroke of the **"e"** suggests a sensitive, defensive ego.

4. The way the words nearly flow into each other shows a desire for logic and order.

5. The big downward loop of the **"g"** indicates a strong libido.

6. The strange curve at the end of the **"d"** shows a probing, possibly kinky personality.

Nov. 2nd 1935

Dear Mr Allen
As you don't read German please bear with my bad English.
I am deep in reading your books, the Case of E. de Vere" first. I have to confess the nerd effect of this study was to increase my doubts and my feelings of bewilderment. I hope I may overcome it. by further reading. but in any case I beg you not to give publicity to my adherence to your views, at least not yet.
Yours most respectfully
Freud

104

sigmund FREUD

Sigmund Freud, the inventor of modern psychoanalysis, launched his career as a neurologist with a focus on "hysteria." Born in 1856, he entered the University of Vienna's Medical School in 1873, and opened a private practice in Vienna in 1886. By the turn of the century he was confronted with the need to prove that many of man's troubles begin in his inner recesses, and he turned the world upside down by publishing "The Interpretation of Dreams." The work pioneered the topic of the unconscious mind, and with it, founded the modern practice of psychoanalysis, based on free association and dream interpretation.

He shocked the world after the turn of the century by popularizing the use of cocaine for medical and psychological purposes, and persuaded a rather uptight society that children indeed had sexuality.

Freud is one of the most influential thinkers of the 20th century. He was famous for asking out loud, as he neared death, "What do women want?"

the handwriting reveals:

- His handwriting shows a person obsessed with sexuality and sensuality.

- However, he is very academically-minded.

- Extremely stressed and had a restless mind, which led to mental exhaustion.

- Tendency for anger and resentment towards authority figures.

philosophers

elie WIESEL

Elie Wiesel, a native of Sighet, Romania, a Hungarian-speaking town in Transylvania, was born in 1928. Young Wiesel was an avid torah scholar and studied the Talmud and Kabbalah with Chasidic rabbis for most of his young life. In 1944, when Wiesel was sixteen, the Nazis deported the fifteen thousand Jews of Sighet to Auschwitz. Wiesel was forced to endure the horror of watching his father die a slow death from disease and starvation. That memory was seared into the young man's mind.

From 1948 to 1951, Wiesel attended the Sorbonne, studied philosophy, and worked as a journalist. One of the most vital parts of Wiesel's career was devoted to bringing the Holocaust to the attention of the public and holding the surviving Nazi's accountable for the atrocities they committed. He taught at New York University from 1972 to 1976 and at Yale University in 1982 and 1983. Wiesel has since published over 30 books, earned the Nobel Peace Prize, chaired the President's Commission on the Holocaust, and was awarded the Congressional Gold Medal of Achievement.

the handwriting reveals:

- He is very intelligent but may be mistrustful and ambivalent in his relationships.
- Much of the time down he has a tendency to feel lonely.
- Distinctive, charismatic, dynamic personality.
- He suffers emotional turmoil but he often covers it up with external aloofness.

Nobel Peace Prize winner who sought out the truths behind the Jewish Holocaust and told the world.

1. The large opening at the bottom of the **"D"** and **"B"** shows a thirst for knowledge not only about the world, but also about himself.

2. The tight left-hand margins are indicative of a suspicious personality bruised by childhood trauma.

3. The open top of the **"a"** marks a person who is talkative.

4. When an **"m"** looks like a "u," the writer is often friendly and kind.

5. The wavy baseline indicates emotional turmoil and instability.

6. Disconnected letters suggest a person who is subject to spontaneous thoughts.

7. The stark, stick-like **"I"** shows an above-average intelligence and straightforwardness.

Dear Mr. Bullan —

Thanks for your letter —

Racism is growing. As is antisemitism. Both must be eradicated. How? I believe in education —

Elie Wiesel

107

A world-renown expert on Jewish Mishna.

1. Very small handwriting, suggesting an analytical mind with strong orientation to details.

2. The **"i"** dash is very long indicating a strong need to explore his own consciousness.

3. The **"g"** loop is so long and deep, showing an ability to connect to subconscious material with a strong, penetrating mind.

4. The base line is very wavy denoting a strong emotional reaction to some kind of inner turmoil.

5. An elongated **"p"** indicates deep motivation to reach high into the spiritual realm.

I pray all the time wherever I go I'am . I dont feel anything during mass . 7/24

Longing to Love God = Love itself.

adin STEINSALTZ

Talmudic scholar Adin Steinsaltz was born in Jerusalem in 1937 into a non-religious family, his father, Abraham, a fierce socialist. Steinsaltz graduated from Jerusalem's Hebrew University, and at age 24, he became the youngest Headmaster in the education system in Israel.

He developed a passion to expose all Jews to the Talmud. In 1965 Steinsaltz founded the Israeli Institute for Talmudic Publications and began work on his massive project of translating and reinterpreting the Talmud. In 1989 he began producing an English edition.

One 1988 poll showed that 84 percent of Israeli Jews still had never read any of it. That same year, Steinsaltz received the Israel Prize, Israel's highest honor, for his work on the Talmud and for furthering Jewish education.

the handwriting reveals:

- Very high level of religiosity.
- Can be vivacious, emotional and warm.

- Humble.
- Extremely analytical and structured.

menachem mendel SCHNEERSON

The Rebbe was born in the Ukraine in 1902 in a prestigious rabbinic family issued from the rebbe of Lyadi, who founded the Lubavitch movement in the 18th Century. He studied Torah in yeshiva and mathematics and science at the University of Berlin and at the Sorbonne in Paris. He arrived in the US during World War II, having escaped first from Germany and then from occupied France. He effectively became the leader of Lubavitch in 1950, after the death of his predecessor and father-in-law, and until his death in 1994.

Under the forty-four year long leadership of Menachem Mendel Schneerson, the Lubavitch hassidic movement grew from a small community nearly devastated by the holocaust to a worldwide organization with more than 200,000 members and one of the most influential forces in world Jewry according to the New York Times. Rabbi Schneerson, called "the Rebbe" by his admirers and followers, spearheaded education and outreach centers in more than thirty countries, including social-service programs open to Jews and non-Jews. Thousands turned to him for advice in person and letters, including other leaders in politics, business, and religion from the US and Israel. Both houses of Congress honored the Rebbe posthumously with the Congressional Gold Medal, mentioning his 'outstanding and lasting contributions toward improvements in world education, morality, and acts of charity."

the handwriting reveals:

• Extremely high level of energy, which denotes powerful leadership ability to push towards goals.

• Used all the resources at his disposal: rest and sleep were too wasteful to him.

• Ability to connect to other people, yet keep his own boundaries and space.

• Fervently religious. No interest in show-off or power races.

The word "impossible" did not exist in the dictionary of the Rebbe of Lubavitch.

1. Deep subconscious exploration.

2. Ability to integrate ancient archetypal material with spiritual elements.

3. High standards in his thinking; need to be exact.

4. Subconscious needs not to mix his intellectual spiritual world with the mundane. Need for clarity of thoughts.

5. Unusual ability to integrate the three levels of high mysticism and spirituality with practical elements and depth psychology. Highly intuitive, bordering on psychic ability.

A rabbi and scholar who defied the Gestapo and the Nazi regime during the Holocaust.

1. The **"n"** is smeared, suggesting a very sensual personality.

2. The **"m"** looks like teeth, indicating a masculine and resolute personality and a great deal of discipline and decisiveness.

3. The **"y"** looks like a hanger, implying a great deal of selectivity and a tendency to chose close friends with care.

4. The **"B"** is open at the bottom, showing an extremely verbal and communicative personality.

5. Extremely small handwriting – a very modest personality, and attentive to details. His concentration level is very high and he has a very deliberate approach to tasks.

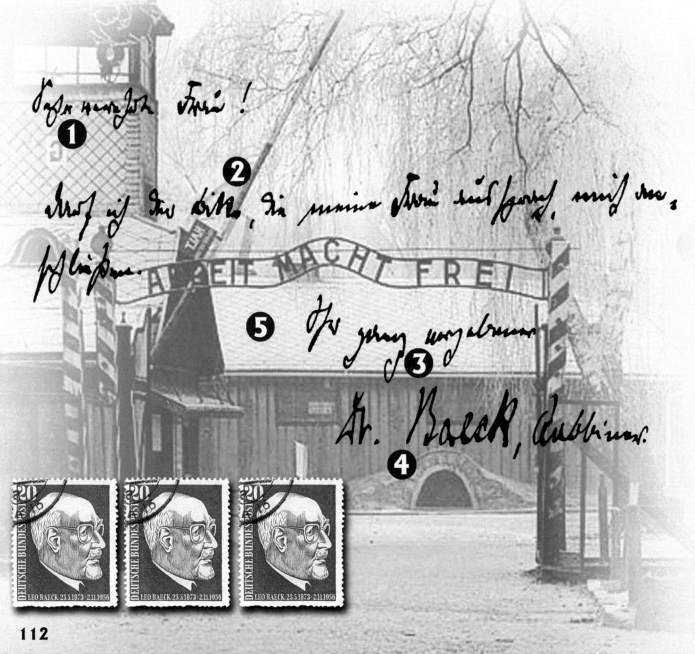

leo BAECK

Polish-born Leo Baeck dedicated a good portion of his life to guiding and supporting the German-Jewish community during the Holocaust. By that time, he was already a revered rabbinical scholar and author of a number of influential books. He served as a rabbi in several German cities, and was in Berlin when the Nazis rose to power in 1933. By that time he was 60, but he chose to stay in Germany and defend Jewish rights. He was twice arrested by the Gestapo but he maintained his course of working to ensure the rights of his people and community were not taken away. As fate would have it, in 1943, at the age of 70, Baeck was deported to Theresienstadt concentration camp.

He miraculously survived and settled in London after the war. In his final years Baeck was chairman of the World Union of Progressive Judaism and taught at the Hebrew Union College in Cincinnati. He died at the age of 83.

the handwriting reveals:

- The handwriting indicates the writer was a powerful motivator who could inspire people and get the best out of them.

- An extroverted, warm personality.

- Very high level of fantasy life, which he used to connect to his religious and spiritual side.

- A deeply insightful personality.

ba'al SHEM TOV

Jews all over the world glorify the name Israel Ben Eliezer, or Ba'al Shem Tov. He was the founder of Chasidism, the revolutionary mystical Jewish lifestyle and worship that took hold in Europe during the 17th century.

Born in Poland to poor and elderly parents, he was orphaned in childhood, and at the tender age of twelve, he taught at a Cheder, a religious elementary school. While in his twenties, his life took a drastic turn as he claimed to have communicated with the biblical prophet Ahijah the Shilonite. He retreated to the Carpathian Mountains, where he lived for seven years in seclusion, working at times as a lime digger. Because of his charisma and insight, he became master and teacher to many Jews. He trained a group of disciples who went on to create the mass movement that defines the beliefs and lives of millions of Jews today.

the handwriting reveals:

- This personality was a genius; one of the most brilliant we have encountered.

- He had a strong sensual side integrated into the religious world.

- A complex and elusive personality.

- A high level of integrity and honesty.

He retreated to Turkey to live in seclusion – and communicate with the prophet Ahija.

1. Hebrew **"Aiyin"** is very looped at the bottom signifying the writer was aware, active and had highly physical drives.

2. Hebrew **"L"** at the top part looks like a canopy, suggesting that he was able to keep thoughts to himself.

3. Hebrew **"shin"** is unusually tall and double looped. It indicates highly evolved spiritual and mystical experiences. The heaviness of the letter indicates that a great deal of emotional enthusiasm is invested in the activity of the mind.

4. The Hebrew **"Aiyin"** is very sharp at the end signifying an unusual way to end the letter and it indicates a vigorous, aggressive attitude toward the world.

The bet ha-midrash of the Ba'al Shem Tov in Medzibezh, Podolia, on a postage stamp issued by the Israeli Post Office in 1960 to commemorate the bicentenary of his death.

115

She grew up in a family that was on the road constantly, and with a mother who was mentally ill.

1. The **"G"** is like a human figure, indicating good concentration with a strong sense of purpose.

2. The **"l"** without a loop shows self-confidence.

3. The **"o"** is filled in indicating she has a high level of sensuality which at times can be aggressive.

4. The **"a"** is open, suggesting someone very talkative.

5. The **"t"** cross bar is in the middle and long, meaning a tendency to be outgoing, influential, magnetic and idealistic. However, it may also indicate a tendency to be number one.

6. The **"m"** looks like thread, suggesting that she may be evasive at times.

gloria STEINEM

Gloria Steinem, one of the most vocal and most published feminists of the 20th century grew up in a family that was constantly on the road. Her mother was mentally ill and held her back from attending school regularly until the age of 10, at which time she also took on the care of her mother, who had become increasingly sick. Steinem found a way to attend school where she excelled in a number of subjects, and graduated from Smith College in 1956, magna cum laude with a degree in government and as a member of Phi Beta Kappa.

She co-founded and wrote for New York magazine at first and later shifted her entire literary focus to the women's liberation movement and explaining the theories of "new feminism." Since then, Steinem has continued to write, speak, and contribute to Ms. Magazine and a long list of other prominent publications. In 1983 she published her first book, "Outrageous Acts and Everyday Rebellions," and in 1986 she published a biography of Marilyn Monroe.

the handwriting reveals:

- She has the personality of a crusader involved in a relentless pursuit of her beliefs.

- Tendency to be a go-getter and not to take prisoners.

- May be very protective of herself, and possibly roundly defeat her opponents.

- A personality with strong opinions and a taste for being in charge.

thinking & IMAGINATION

UPPER ZONE: The upper zone of the various letters is a great source of information regarding intellectual and spiritual activities. It is also an indicator for creative activities. The letters b, d, f, h, j, k, l, and t contain an upper zone. Generally, the taller and fuller the loop, the more emphasis the writer puts on thinking.

On Monday morning I will be going to Boston.

The upper zone is short: meaning self-reliant, realistic and independent. This person shuns intellectualism. The writer is more involved in the "here and now" and the practical endeavors of this world. Don't anticipate too many complex or sophisticated ideas in his stories.

On Friday afternoon I am going

The upper zone is very elaborate: This writer has a very creative mind, a good imagination and is mentally resourceful. If the handwriting is scrawly or illegible, it might be a paranoid schizophrenic or a very disturbed person who can imagine things that don't really exist.

On Friday afternoon I will be

The upper zone is full: The person is a good thinker, very philosophical and open-minded. He is thoughtful, creative and can consider new ideas. He thinks sociologically and has a speculative, hypothetical mind. Spirituality is very important.

As Manager of a $10-15 million annual sales

Flame-like point on the tip: This writer lives in an abstract world and has a great deal of interest in theory and concepts. This person is interested in exploring intellectual concepts and the "upper" realm. Keen imagination is very notable here.

I am flying to England

The upper zones are hyper inflated: Can be a positive sign. This person is creative and has an interest in new concepts. She enjoys ideas that are new and stimulating and can be very tolerant and compromising. This person has a strong ability to visualize and can see the greater possibilities. She is also easy-going about rules and regulations. On the negative side, this person's thinking can be distorted; she could be emotionally touchy and hard on herself. Or, the thinker can be an excessive daydreamer.

Handwriting is an excellent tool to assess the imagination, creativity and thinking process of the writer.

[handwriting sample]

The upper zone looks like a stick and is bowed right: indicating problems in the thinking process. The right side of the written page represents the past. If the past has an overbearing effect on the thinking process, then there is some kind of distortion. There is a tendency to find compromises in the thinking processes.

[handwriting sample]

The upper zone is hooked: showing that the thinker has the desire to possess knowledge, hangs on to ideas, and has mental tenacity. The thinker might be interested in religion and ethics.

DEVIATION FROM COPY BOOK HANDWRITING: We all learn in school how to write in neat and perfect handwriting. As years go by, our personalities and our accumulating life experiences start to change the way we write. Generally there are four major deviations.

On Saturday morning I will be going to Milwaukee to the Palette Shop.

Perfect handwriting: usually indicates a boring, follow the rules personality. This might also point to the writer's need to avoid anxiety or a phobia. His thinking might be limited and/or restricted in order to repress an anxious subconscious.

On Tuesday morning I will be going to St. Louis to Boatmen's Tower.

Normal variation from the copybook handwriting: shows a more complex personality is being formed. This writing reveals a person who is not afraid to express himself and his individuality. He is not overly bound by rigid social rules.

[handwriting sample]

Pathological variation from the copybook: usually severe criminals, abnormal personalities, or medically unfit people. They cannot get their facts straight, and they have elaborate idiosyncratic ideation. Their disturbances are noticeable after spending a short amount of time with them.

Ben Shahn

Creative variation of the copybook handwriting: like Ben Shahn, the handwriting is still legible, yet has a creative flair to it. The writer has an ability to see things in a more elaborate and complex way. This is a positive sign, as he is able to translate those visions to acceptable social norms.

Jews & Money

Almost as long as Jews have been dispersed throughout Europe, other cultures have accused and persecuted Jews for monetary gains. Conspiracy theories have flourished to this day, accusing Jews of controlling the entire banking system, and sometimes entire governments. Although these accusations are vastly untrue, every myth usually has just an ounce of legitimacy or truth.

It is true that there are many wealthy Jews. Look at the Forbes 500 richest people list. Michael Eisner, David Geffen, the Rothschilds, Steven Spielberg, Bronfman are just a couple at the top of the list. Furthermore, 61% of Nobel Prize winners in Economics are Jews. Let's look at some of the possible reasons:

Limitations that drove them to succeed
For generations, gentiles did not let the Jews join any trade organization or buy land. They saw the Jews as a foreign entity unworthy of intermingling with. That left no choice for the Jews but to deal in trade with whatever monies or goods they arrived with; money exchange.

Usury and Jews: The written Torah prohibits usury, but rabbis have found ways to make some forms of money lending legal. Like other material resources, money can become sacred if its use promotes God's plans for the world. Wealth presents people with precious opportunities for themselves, their families, loved-ones and others in the world who are not as fortunate. God blessed Abraham with great wealth and many possessions. What was good enough for the first Jew is certainly good enough for all his descendants!

We also know that the first economist in the Bible was Joseph, the son of Jacob. His intuitive sensibilities enabled him to forecast the future and help create the wealth of the Pharaohs. He predicted the famine and filled the storage houses with grain. He ran the Egyptian economy. Being one of the first sons of Judaism, it became evident that wealth and money management is embedded in the Jewish tradition.

Tzedaka – Charity – Giving back....
An extremely important factor in the Jewish faith, (which is also one of the Ten Commandments), is "tzedaka," charity, giving to those in need. In order to fulfill this command you must have wealth of some kind. So wealth creation was encouraged in order to fulfill the Jewish commandments and to ensure those with money would help those without it.

Kadman Numismatic Museum Collection, Museum Haaretz, Tel-Aviv

Jewish National Fund donation boxes,
Israel and USA, 1930s-1980s.
Tamar Talisman Collection, Tel-Aviv

"Whoever loves money never has money enough; whoever loves wealth is never satisfied with his income."

Ecclesiastes 5:10

entrepreneurs

monica LEWINSKY

This young woman, famous for her controversial relationship with President Bill Clinton, was born in San Francisco and graduated with a degree in psychology. Soon thereafter, she eagerly accepted an unpaid internship at the White House. In January of 1998, Linda Tripp revealed she had tapes of Lewinsky and President Bill Clinton talking about an illicit affair. During the investigation that followed, the country learned that parts of this affair could have taken place in the Oval Office.

Lewinsky was granted immunity from prosecution in exchange for her testimony. She ended up as the center of a political scandal that focused on having the president impeached.

She told her story in the 1999 book "Monica's Story," written by Andrew Morton. After a brief sabbatical from the public eye, she became a handbag designer and during part of 2003, she hosted the Fox show "Mr. Personality."

the handwriting reveals:

- Emotionally unstable personality.

- Ambitious, outgoing, and assertive.

- Deep down, however, she may not be so sophisticated.

- Possibly reckless and "clueless."

The woman who nearly brought
a U.S. President to impeachment.

1. The first bump of the **"m"** is higher, indicating an ambitious personality.

2. The big loop in the lower zone of the **"j"** is a sign of materialism.

3. The long arms and feet of the **"I"** (like the Roman numeral) suggest someone who is caring in her relationships.

4. The sharp end stroke of the **"Y"** shows tenacity.

5. The cross bar almost directly in the middle of the **"t"** indicates the writer is practical and down-to-earth.

6. The long end stroke on the loop in the **"y"** is indicative of a vigorous sensual personality.

7. The sharp summit in the **"h"** also suggests a tendency towards assertiveness.

8. The sweeping cross bar in the **"A"** indicates a tendency to be a natural entertainer.

next time we come can join us. I would with your class at Nathan's

All the best,
monica Lewinsky

One of the most powerful investors in this country's history.

1. The capital **"B"** is inflated, suggesting an inflated ego, also a bluffer.

2. The **"B"** is open at the base, meaning talkative.

3. The **"e"** looks like "i" indicating Mr. Baruch had a very keen mind, but was secretive.

4. The **"n"** is wavy, indicating changeability and adeptness at diplomacy.

5. The **"a"** is open, also meaning a tendency to be very verbal.

6. The **"r"** is very pointed: a perceptive and probing mind.

7. The **"h"** is angular and high-looped signifying an aggressive mind at work.

UNFORGETTABLE BERNARD BARUCH

124

bernard BARUCH

Little Orphan Annie's Daddy Warbucks was fashioned after Bernard Mannes Baruch, one of the most powerful financiers and investors in the history of America. His father, Simon, was a physician. His mother, Belle, was American-born from a family of South Carolina plantation owners.

His family moved to New York in 1881. Baruch attended public school, and enrolled in the City College of New York. His first job was in druggist's glassware, but Wall Street dazzled him and reeled him in.

By the time Baruch was 26, a powerful stockbroker offered him an eighth of interest in his firm and Baruch's trading career began to skyrocket. By the age of 30, Baruch had achieved millionaire status with an uncanny ability to predict the movements of stocks. After the 1918 armistice, Baruch became an economic advisor to President Wilson at the Paris Peace Conference. He died at the age of 95 in 1965.

the handwriting reveals:

- A huge ego, but it didn't show outwardly.

- A very private personality who showed just enough to come across as likeable.

- Submerged beneath the surface was a big authority problem; he yielded to no one.

- At times a strong sense of vanity that fed on the admiration of others.

helena RUBINSTEIN

Born in Krakow, Poland, Helena Rubinstein, the world's first "beauty mogul," was a businesswoman from the start, as a teenager she served as her father's bookkeeper and had a hand in running his business. Then her mother's friend, a famous actress of her time, introduced her to the world of beauty and fashion. After refusing to marry a designated man chosen by her father, she moved to Australia. Many Australian women suffered from sun-damaged skin; and it wasn't long before Rubinstein had given away almost all of the Modjeska cream she had brought with her from Poland.

In 1890 she opened her first shop. Eight years later, the shops had become wildly successful and she began to expand the business, adding products and opening salons in London and Paris. In 1915 she moved to New York City and opened a salon there. By 1917 she had salons in most major North American cities. By the time she died, in 1965, at the age of 94, she'd become queen of a worldwide beauty empire.

the handwriting reveals:

- Possible tendency to be relentless in her preoccupations.

- Sharp and tough.

- Channeled her sensuality into business.

- Tendency towards expressing herself in a very vigorous way and handle opponents in a firm way.

The world's first "beauty mogul," was a businesswoman from the start; and she knew what women wanted.

1. The right slant of the signature reflects an outgoing, vivacious, social personality.

2. The "l" is tall with a narrow loop which indicates that she is an ambitious personality who is able to control her own thinking process and emotional subconscious.

3. The "n" has two sharp points meaning that she can be very sharp, analytical thinker who has a no-nonsense approach to problem solving and interpersonal intimacy.

4. The "t" cross bar is very long and moderately high which signifies that she is a very energetic, powerful and task-oriented personality who is able to be practical enough to carry through her business ventures.

5. The "i" dot is high and forward, suggesting that the writer has a great deal of imagination and is resistant to slow down her quick thinking processes. This is an excellent indicator of a visionary entrepreneur.

One of the founders of the Hollywood Dream

1. The **"T"** cross bar is hooked, meaning a strong, determined personality with action-oriented, highly motivated and strong, optimistic views.

2. The **"a"** is open at the top, indicating someone who is talkative and open to new ideas.

3. The **"d"** has a full loop, suggesting sensitivity to criticism.

4. The **"8"** is open at the top, suggesting a subconscious need to be free and not be controlled by any one.

5. The **"f"** has no upper zone or hook, suggesting that Jack was a great observer of people.

6. The beginning stroke of the **"S"** starts below the baseline indicating a cautious personality.

7. The **"r"** is pointed, indicating a penetrating mind.

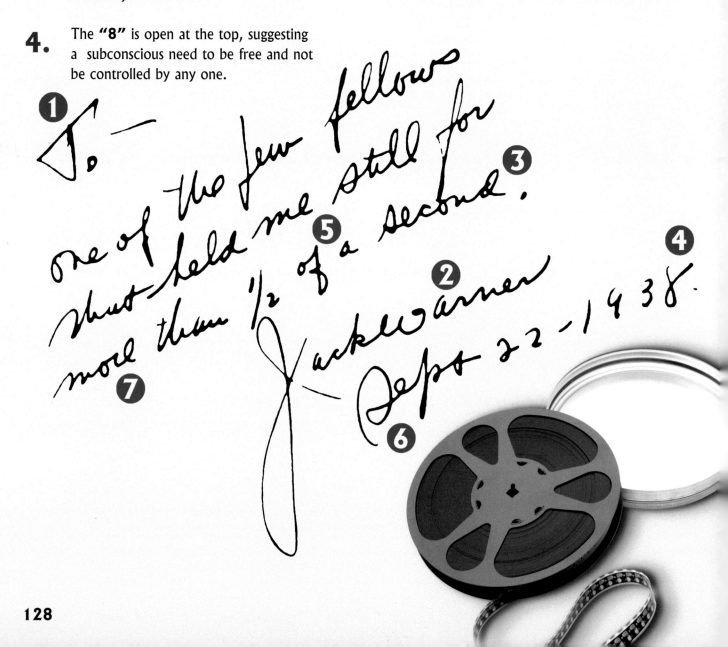

jack WARNER

Jack L. Warner was born in 1892 to Polish immigrants, who bought a nickelodeon in Newcastle, Pennsylvania. Jack sang to entertain the audience during intermission. In 1905 four of the Warner brothers ventured into film distribution, and later took their first stab at production with a series of not-too-successful shorts.

Their first success was with "My Four Years in Germany" (1917) and subsequently they were able to establish Warner Brothers Pictures. Jack ran the studio with a firm and frugal hand, and was famous for his hawkish political views and occasional tactless cracks. He often clashed with his producers and writers.

To Einstein, he once quipped: "I have a theory of relatives too. Don't hire 'em."

In 1956, Harry and Albert Warner sold most of their shares in the company, but Jack stayed on as studio boss and largest single stockholder. In 1967 he sold his interest in Warner Brothers to Seven Arts and became an independent producer.

the handwriting reveals:

- He tried very hard to control his unstable emotional side.

- Warm and generous.

- Very religious, spiritual person, as opposed to the businessman image he portrayed in his everyday life.

- Extremely developed critical skills.

ben STEIN

Ben Stein wears many hats and can be classified as the "drollest of the droll" of Jewish comedians. On top of that, he's an attorney, a commentator, respected columnist, author, sometime actor and talk show host and an intellectual with impeccable Washington credentials. He followed in his father's footsteps, Herbert Stein, who was a noted economist with ties to the White House throughout his career.

Ben grew up in the D.C. area, graduated from Columbia with honors in economics and from Yale Law School in 1970 as valedictorian. As a lawyer, he worked for the poor, for the Federal Trade Commission and at the White House. He wrote speeches for Richard Nixon and Gerald Ford.

He has written 16 books with titles like "A License to Steal," "Michael Milken and the Conspiracy to Bilk the Nation" and "The View from Sunset Boulevard." His part as the boring teacher in "Ferris Bueller's Day Off" has been ranked as one of the 50 most famous scenes in American film. In July of 1997, he became the host of the Comedy Central quiz show, "Win Ben Stein's Money," and has served as a celebrity judge on the CBS show, "Star Search."

the handwriting reveals:

- Very clever personality.

- High sense of pride and not likely to bow to any authority figure.

- Some sense of vanity and pompousness.

- Underneath a boring facade lies a very high-end sense of humor

The "drollest of the droll" of Jewish comedians.

1. The handwriting slant is straight (90 degrees), indicating a highly focused person who likes to call the shots and marches according to his inner drummer.

2. The handwriting is disconnected – implying that he lets himself stay in tune with his intuition.

3. The **"B"** has a large opening at the bottom, showing a strong need for self knowledge.

4. The **"in"** in the signature – a good indicator of someone who is willing to be diplomatic and might not always reveal the whole story.

5. The **"S"** is encircled, suggesting a good imagination and sense of humor.

Jews & The People of the Book

The Jews have been termed, "The People of the Book," with "The Book" meaning one thing: the Bible (or Torah). The saying stems from the nature of Judaism and its commandments, in particular the one prohibiting the making and worshipping of idol images. Because of it, the Jews resorted to studying the written word, after all, the Ten Commandments were written on stone.

Thus began the tradition of scribes and intense study of the scriptures. Folklore and written words have always wielded tremendous power in Judaism. The ancient Kabala deals with the power of words.

Another command is to "read the Bible day and night." Jews were trained from age three to read. Reading became second nature to the jewish nation. Further proof to the power of words can be found in daily religious rituals. Traditional Jews wear Teffilin on their head and forehead: Teffilin is a holy scroll in a leather box and worn on the forehead and left hand every day of the week. It symbolizes the connection to God.

The tradition of "The Book" has produced a large number of Nobel Prize-winning authors. Included are:

- 1910 **Paul Heyse**
- 1927 **Henri Bergson**
- 1958 **Boris Pasternak**
- 1966 **Shmuel Yosef Agnon**
- 1966 **Nelly Sachs**
- 1976 **Saul Bellow**
- 1978 **Isaac Bashevis Singer**
- 1987 **Joseph Brodsky**
- 1991 **Nadine Gordimer**
- 2005 **Harold Pinter**

"I have hidden your word in my heart that I might not sin against you. Praise be to you, O Lord; teach me your decrees With my lips I recount all the laws that come from your mouth."

Psalm 119:11-12

"Torah Studies;" etching by Ben Uri, 1940

A Torah scribe

writers

7

Her mother once said "God knows everything: Anne knows everything better."

1. The **"h"** is looped, indicating that she had intellectual and spiritual needs, plus good creativity.

2. The **"m"** looks like a tooth, signaling a very disciplined and energetic writer. High intelligence.

3. The **"F"** is smeared, indicating strong emotional needs.

4. The **"g"** lower loop is full indicating an awareness of her physical needs.

5. The **"i"** dot lies close and above the stem; indicates a very punctual and precise writer.

1945-1929

1939

anne FRANK

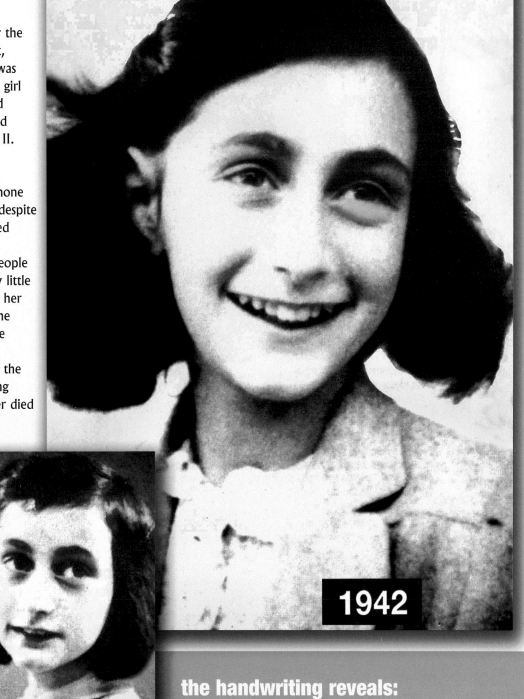

1942

Over one million children under the age of sixteen died in the Holocaust, Anne Frank was one of them. She was fifteen years old – a tragic end to a girl who was an impish, happy child and whose diary became a best-seller and revered stage play after World War II. Her mother once said "God knows everything; Anne knows everything better." The girl's self-confidence shone throughout the pages of her diary, despite the misery and terror that dominated their existence during the Nazi occupation. She was one of eight people living in cramped quarters with very little food and no escape. She recounted her life faithfully for two years before the Nazis found and deported her entire family.

The diary was later found among the ruins of her family's ransacked hiding place in Amsterdam. Anne's mother died January 6, 1945, at Auschwitz-Birkenau seven months after they were arrested. Only two months before the camp was liberated, Anne Frank and her older sister, Margot, died of typhus in 1945 at Bergen-Belsen.

the handwriting reveals:

- Outgoing, extroverted personality who was able to make friends easily.

- Good conversationalist and communicator.

- Tendency towards occasional emotional outbursts.

- Highly ambitious and curious.

135

isaac ASIMOV

Isaac Asimov's family arrived in the United States through Ellis Island, settled in Brooklyn in the early 20s, and ran a candy store. He was already writing stories at the Boys High School of Brooklyn – but his official career took off in the direction of chemistry, in which he majored at Columbia. After serving in World War II he earned his Ph.D. in the same field. All the while, however, he kept publishing, beginning with the sci-fi novel "Marooned off Vesta," in 1939. Even while he was teaching at Boston University School of Medicine, his passion took him ever deeper into science fiction. He, at the same time, was phenomenally successful as a writer of science books for the general public.

Before his death in 1992, Asimov commented, "I'm on fire to explain, and happiest when it's something reasonably intricate which I can make clear step by step." He also discovered that he was a most able and entertaining lecturer who delighted in his work as a teacher.

the handwriting reveals:

- A very colorful personality, but emotionally unstable.

- High anxiety with irritable moods, accompanied by exaggerated needs for self-protection.

- Problems concentrating; seems to be easily distracted by unimportant events.

- The handwriting indicates a person who did not have an easy childhood.

"I'm on fire to explain, and happiest when it's something reasonably intricate which I can make clear, step by step." – Isaac Asimov

1. The **"I"** has an extension to the left signifying severe father issues.

2. The **"I"** has a tall and full loop suggesting high sensitivity to criticism.

3. The **"a"** is knotted inside: usually means the writer was secretive and likely to deceive himself.

4. The **"A"** is full and knotted at the bottom: meaning a warm, loving personality, with strong needs to be pampered, but the writer can be irritable if under pressure.

5. The **"v"** end stroke is high, suggesting a tendency to use love as a bridge to other people.

MATERIALISM

go home

Dominant lower zone with inflated loops: These people not only have a healthy sexual appetite (which is of course a materialistic variable) but also have a love of material and financial passions. They have a strong interest in money and are resourceful in acquiring it.

I yearn for $.

They like to start from scratch and build their wealth. They enjoy travel and excitement and make good entrepreneurs. They are ambitious and therefore can risk investing money in the stock market. They love comfort and good food and work hard to get it.

I love how it feels

Pasty and smeared handwriting: This person needs material possessions. He likes to feel, touch and experience things. The smell, texture and look of an object is very important to him. However, he is more likely to be messy, inconsiderate of his possessions and more in need of buying new items to replenish the old.

2 am 8am

Some letters written as figures: This style of writing indicates a person who is interested in numbers. He is frugal and economical, and uses all resources at hand. He lets the importance of numbers penetrate into his subconscious.

please come today and bring us

Narrow margins or no margins at all: This writer is a person who uses money wisely; he might empty the refrigerator completely before buying groceries. Such writers will think twice before purchasing new clothes.

I love money

Short, clipped end strokes: shows a very impulsive person and a big spender. This writer has a low level of restraint; typically an impulsive person who acts without first processing the consequences of his or her actions.

One of the most important indications is the lower zone. Most of us are conditioned from early childhood to view heaven as a spiritual world high and above us, the earthly zone as earthy practicality and the lower zone as sexuality and materialistic. Those archetypes are imprinted on our mind and infuse themselves subconsciously into our handwriting. Visualize a bag of money – then look at the bottom of a "g."

WHERE are you

Simplified: Most of the time, simplicity represents a simple taste in material items. The clothes are simpler, the car is less eye-catching, and so forth. This writer's materialistic needs are not extravagant or flashy, but are functional and basic.

I am economical

Small Size: Usually, small handwriting indicates analytical and rational thinking. This writer is more likely to be economical. She would think twice before making any purchases and she is less likely to be lavish with her expenditures.

I am not frugal

Narrowness: describes the width of letters and the spacing between them. The more letters that occupy a line of handwriting, the more frugal a person is. This example shows a writer who is not frugal. He likes to expand his handwriting which is indicated by the wide letters and larger amount of space between each letter.

how are you today

Pasty, thick lines: This writer always needs more "stuff." The more he buys, the more he needs. A good example is someone who buys compulsively on the television shopping channels. There is a great need to hoard more and more merchandise.

Elizabeth

Inflated figures: This writer is more likely to be extravagant in her spending. She is the opposite of the simplified example earlier. Materialistically, those glitzy, over-priced gadgets are right down her alley. This extravagant side is an extension of her inner need for attention and admiration from others.

I hate giving $

Hooks on starting or end strokes: This means the writer cannot let go of money, and is more likely to be a miser. From an early age he was trained to feel that losing things will bring him anxiety. Freud would also say that he might have some anal retentive traits.

The Fear of Flying Factor.

1. The capital **"T"** is convex and joined to the next letter, suggesting a passive desire to be the center of attention.

2. The **"n"** looks like teeth: indicates she can sometimes become very aggressive, and she might be very aggressive verbally.

3. The **"k"** is open and looped, suggesting an energetic, go-getter personality.

4. The **"h"** upper loop is full. Indicates a very sensual personality.

5. The **"g"** is like a cork, meaning a passionate personality with a hot temper.

6. The **"o"** with inside loop is associated with a tendency to have illusions.

7. The capital **"J"**, upper part, is looped, a sign of high creativity and sensitivity.

8. The **"a"** is smeared and messy, suggesting a tendency for sexual preoccupation and addiction.

9. The sharp upper zone of the **"E"** suggests a very quick mind and love of culture.

Thank you so much!
Erica Jones

erica JONG

Erica Jong, writer and poet, was born in New York City and studied at Barnard College (1963 BA) and Columbia University (1965 MA; School of Fine Arts 1969-70). She taught at a variety of institutions throughout New York City, and in Heidelberg, Germany, as a faculty member of the Overseas Division of the University of Maryland. She wrote volumes of poetry and novels, and achieved celebrity status with her 1973 bestseller, "Fear of Flying: A Novel," a story of sexual fantasies that some interpret as a liberating text for women.

the handwriting reveals:

- Strong need for self-indulgence.

- Poetic, with a roller coaster personality.

- Very high intelligence, accompanied by a very penetrating, critical personality.

- Self-centered.

isaac bashevis SINGER

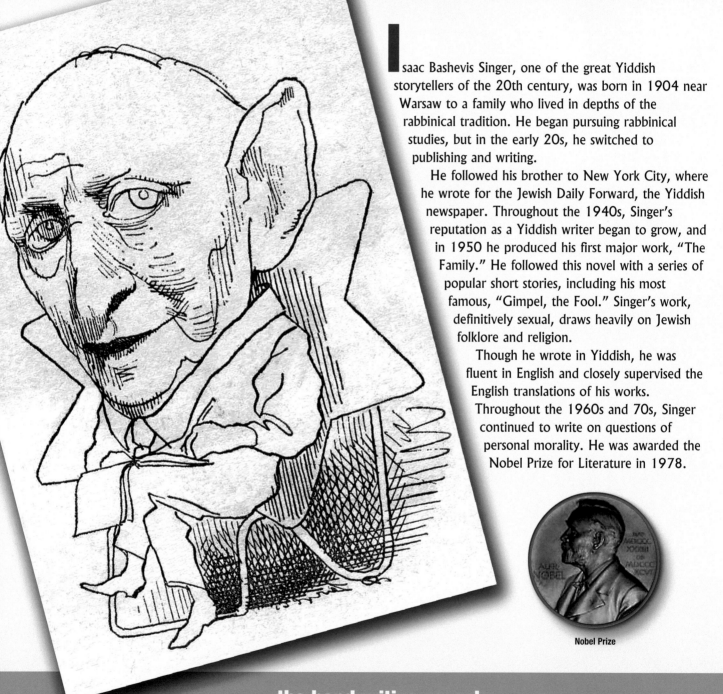

Isaac Bashevis Singer, one of the great Yiddish storytellers of the 20th century, was born in 1904 near Warsaw to a family who lived in depths of the rabbinical tradition. He began pursuing rabbinical studies, but in the early 20s, he switched to publishing and writing.

He followed his brother to New York City, where he wrote for the Jewish Daily Forward, the Yiddish newspaper. Throughout the 1940s, Singer's reputation as a Yiddish writer began to grow, and in 1950 he produced his first major work, "The Family." He followed this novel with a series of popular short stories, including his most famous, "Gimpel, the Fool." Singer's work, definitively sexual, draws heavily on Jewish folklore and religion.

Though he wrote in Yiddish, he was fluent in English and closely supervised the English translations of his works. Throughout the 1960s and 70s, Singer continued to write on questions of personal morality. He was awarded the Nobel Prize for Literature in 1978.

Nobel Prize

the handwriting reveals:

- A charming personality who knew how to endear himself to other people.

- Could be somewhat manipulative at times.

- Showed paranoid tendencies and a high degree of mistrust

- A huge, overwhelming ego.

Singer's work, often frankly sexual, draws heavily on Jewish folklore, religion, and mysticism.

1. The **"G"** is open showing a good, analytical mind with great creativity. It also indicates a good appetite and liking for food.

2. The space between the capital **"G"** and the **"r"** shows a somewhat cautious person.

3. The **"i"** dot is missing indicating a good imagination, plus a tendency to want to keep moving and "get on with it."

4. The very full upper zone of the **"S"** shows a very highly cultured personality, someone eager to work with his imagination – at the expense of practicality.

5. The **"r"** is concave, which could mean a need for higher inspiration, for getting to a higher state of being.

6. The **"B"** is open and hooked at the base, suggesting three things: egoism, a need to conceal, along with a talkative personality.

7. The Personal Pronoun **"I"** is 7 round, suggesting that he is friendly to his past and a tendency to need flattery.

He launched himself in Paris, and became one of the most widely syndicated columnists ever.

1. The **"i"** dot is very high: lots of imagination.

2. The **"i"** dot is a dash signifying an impatient and critically penetrating mind.

3. The **"t"** cross bar takes off to the right suggesting an aggressive approach to any given situation or problem.

4. Stem of the **"d"** is sharp, suggesting a tendency towards cynicism, a good sense of humor, and, again, a penetrating mind.

5. The **"a"** is smudged implying a great deal of sensuality; it also can indicate explosive anger.

6. The **"B"** is open at the base line, suggesting that he was talkative and had a great desire for self knowledge.

in Zivil: Art Buchwald

art BUCHWALD

Art Buchwald, son of a curtain manufacturer, was born in 1925 in Mt. Vernon, New York and grew up in Queens. He left high school at 17 to join the Marines and served through World War II. He used the GI Bill to go to college, and moved to Paris after graduation. In January 1949, he took a sample column to the Paris office of the New York Herald Tribune, titled "Paris After Dark," it was filled with scraps of offbeat information about Parisian nightlife. He was hired, and his columns began to recruit readers on both sides of the Atlantic.

He returned to the United States in 1962; and his column appeared in some 300 newspapers from Enid, Oklahoma, to Israel. Buchwald has written over 30 books including "Leaving Home," "I'll Always Have Paris," and "I think I Don't Remember." He won the Pulitzer Prize for Outstanding Commentary in 1982. He died in 2005.

the handwriting reveals:

- Outgoing, go-getter personality.

- Sarcastic, imaginative and sharp.

- Has a great need for sanity and mental order.

- A tenacious and dedicated personality.

arthur MILLER

Growing up on the streets of Harlem since his birth in 1915, Arthur Miller is without a doubt one of the leading American playwrights of the 20th century. As a child, he was barely conscious of being Jewish, but he learned early how tough life could be. His father was a coat manufacturer who was financially ruined during the Depression. By the time he reached the age of 13, the family had moved to Brooklyn. Determined to go to college, he worked in an auto parts warehouse for two years to save up tuition, and studied playwriting at the University of Michigan. He broke into Broadway with "The Man Who Had All the Luck" (1944). It closed after only four performances, but he went on to garner critical acclaim for his novel "Focus" and the play "All My Sons." Probably his most important work, "Death of a Salesman" (1949) was an immediate success and won him the Pulitzer Prize and a second Drama Critics Award.

He became a father figure to Marilyn Monroe with whom he fell madly in love and married. He died in 2005.

the handwriting reveals:

- Outgoing personality with a domineering, complex presence.

- He may be disorganized and messy.

- Extremely sensitive and vulnerable personality; impatient.

- Strong need for being loved.

Probably his most important work, "Death of a Salesman" (1949) was an immediate success and won him the Pulitzer Prize and a second Drama Critics Award.

1. The **"y"** loop is straight and slanted to the right. It may be associated with a tendency for assertiveness and aggression. Maintains an interest in his fellow man.

2. The **"t"** trends upward indicating action oriented, good aspirations and imaginative.

3. The **"p"** is rounded and looped in the starting stroke, which may indicate a tendency to not always tell the truth.

4. The handwriting has a right slant, meaning outgoing: wants to connect with people.

5. The **"d"** is looped, indicating a tendency to be overly emotional.

6. The starting stroke of the **"M"** has a large circle, which can be associated with a tendency towards possessiveness with other people.

"Neil has the ability to write characters – even the leading characters that we're supposed to root for – that are absolutely flawed." – Jack Lemon

1. The rounded, descending leg of the **"p"** signals a writer that is unafraid of bluffing to secure advantage.

2. The wide loops on the **"d"** and the **"t"** indicate a sensitive, vulnerable personality.

3. The intersected **"o"** suggests a person who tries hard to control his emotions. He's not always sincere.

4. The floating dot on the **"i"** indicates a quick-thinker with a strong sense of curiosity.

5. The sharp hump on the **"N"** shows an ambitious personality.

6. The high dot over the **"i"** suggests an imaginative person whose thoughts are often in the clouds.

neil SIMON

Born on July 4, 1927, Neil Simon grew up in Washington Heights in Manhattan. He started out as a reporter for the U.S. Army. Once discharged, he took a job as a mail room clerk at Warner Brothers' New York office. With help from his older brother Danny, he got some connections in the business.

He became part of the legendary team of writers for Sid Caesar's "Your Show of Shows," which employed some of the best comic minds in television. Among them were Mel Brooks, Woody Allen, Larry Gelbart and Carl Reiner. Later he began writing for himself, his first hit as a playwright being 1961's "Come Blow Your Horn." He had an unparalleled string of successes in the 60s, including "Barefoot in the Park," "The Odd Couple" and "Star-Spangled Girl." He has been showered with more Academy and Tony nominations than any other writer, and is the only playwright to have four Broadway productions running simultaneously.

the handwriting reveals:

- A great observer and a good listener.
- Tendency to easily stress out.
- Great sense of humor.
- Highly ambitious.

writers

philip ROTH

Philip Roth was born in Newark, New Jersey, in 1933 during the Depression era. After graduating from the University of Chicago with an M.A. in English, he joined the army in 1955 but was discharged soon after. His national award-winning book, "Goodbye, Columbus," his first novel, was published in 1959. In 1969, his seminal best-seller "Portnoy's Complaint" hit the stands. The book was a huge and controversial success, delving into sexuality to a degree that prompted condemnations from rabbis and other figures in the Jewish community.

He has earned numerous awards, including the National Book Award (1995 for "Sabbath Theater") and two PEN/Faulkner Awards (1993 and 2000). Roth married English actress Claire Bloom in 1990, but their marriage ended messily in 1995. His 2000 novel "The Human Stain" was recently adapted as a film starring Anthony Hopkins and Nicole Kidman.

the handwriting reveals:

- Passionate and inflamed personality, laced with forceful urges.

- A mind that wanders and is possessed with infatuated needs.

- Mentally adventurous and breaks through the imagination barrier.

- Sexually preoccupied.

"Portnoy's Complaint" was a huge controversial success, and it unleashed rabid condemnations from rabbis and other figures in the Jewish community.

1. The full descender from the **"P"** shows a practical, self-reliant person.

2. The soaring **"Ph"** (as well as the full descending **"p"** at the end of his name) indicates both idealism and frequent thoughts related to sensuality.

3. The high, full **"l"** suggests a tendency to deal with aggression via writing and thinking.

4. The floating dot of the **"i"** suggests a person with a tremendous imagination, someone who is capable of taking flights of fantasy.

5. The crippled **"R"** indicates a person who likes to be on top of things much of the time.

6. The jagged tip formed by the **"t"** and the **"h"** suggests a person full of criticism.

Lazarus had the greatest renown among Jewish-American female poets and writers.

1. The upper zone of the **"E"** is enriched, meaning generosity and idealism.

2. The **"L"** with no upper loop, suggesting a positive attitude, but also materialistic.

3. The **"r"** shows a very sharp personality, which would not likely expose her inner self.

4. The handwriting is very heavily smeared, suggesting a strong, sensual personality.

The New Colossus

Not like the brazen giant of Greek fame,

With conquering limbs astride from land to land;

Here at our sea-washed, sunset gates shall stand

A mighty woman with a torch, whose flame

Is the imprisoned lightening, and her name

Mother of Exiles. From her beacon-hand

Glows world-wide welcome; her mild eyes command

The air-bridged harbor that twin cities frame.

"Keep ancient lands, your storied pomp!" cries she

With silent lips. "Give me your tired, your poor,

Your huddled masses yearning to breathe free,

The wretched refuse of your teeming shore.

Send these, the homeless, tempest-tost to me,

I lift my lamp beside the golden door!"

Sonnet by Emma Lazarus,1883. Engraved onto a plaque on the Statue of Liberty's pedestal in 1903.

emma LAZARUS

Of all Jewish female poets and writers in 19th century America, Emma Lazarus was the most famous. Born in 1849 to a wealthy sugar merchant, she grew up in a privileged household in New York and Newport, Rhode Island, and was educated by private tutors.

It was in her 30s that she truly flowered. In addition to numerous magazine poems, essays, and letters, she published a highly respected volume of translations, "Poems and Ballads of Heinrich Heine," in 1881, and "Songs of a Semite: The Dance to Death and Other Poems," in 1882. Soon after "Poems and Translations" were published, Lazarus met Ralph Waldo Emerson. The two corresponded until Emerson's death in 1882. But her career was cut short. In 1887, Lazarus returned to New York from Europe very ill, probably with cancer. She died two months later. Two of Lazarus' sisters published "The Poems of Emma Lazarus, I and II" posthumously, in 1888.

the handwriting reveals:

- A highly imaginative person.

- She may have been emotionally immature.

- Withdrawn into her own inner world.

- But with a great love of life. Tendency for sensuality.

barbara WALTERS

From childhood, Barbara Walters had an advantage toward becoming a celebrity interviewer. Her father, Lew Walters, was an influential Broadway producer and owner of the Latin Quarter night club. Her young life, split between New York City and Miami, was filled with celebrity encounters of all kinds.

After college, she took off to New York to begin a career in television. She started in public relations at RCA-TV. In 1961 she went to work for the "Today" show. By 1963 her interviews had become a regular feature on "Today," but it took her nine years to rise to co-anchor. Her early career moves helped pave the way for women in U.S. network news.

One of her greatest achievements was the 1976 joint interview with Anwar Sadat and Menachem Begin just before their meeting in Jerusalem. She then went on to co-host "20/20" and launched a series of specials dedicated to celebrity interviews. She is famous for her daring and probing line of questioning, which sometimes pushes the envelope for audiences around the world.

the handwriting reveals:

- Relentless. Tendency to cut every corner to achieve her goals.

- A strong sense of being right in every argument; the ability to attack those who oppose her.

- May have a strong need to control her emotions.

- Tendency to be tough.

One of her greatest achievements: the 1976 joint interview with Anwar Sadat and Menachem Begin just before their meeting in Jerusalem.

1. The **"B"** is open, indicating a talkative personality.

2. The **"s"** is totally locked, suggesting a tendency to be in control.

3. The **"a"** is open, indicating a tendency for being a big schmoozer.

4. The **"a"** end stroke looks like a knife suggesting that behind the smiling face there is a person who can give you a fight.

5. The **"t"** cross bar is in the middle: a very practical personality.

knowing WHOM to avoid

There are times in our lives when we wish we had known the real modus operandi of a person who ends up being nothing but trouble. Lets talk about utterly dishonest people – the ones who steal from you, leave you holding the bag or cause you damage. Their handwriting generally will give you an advanced warning. Although it is hard to be totally sure, here are some clues to help you recognize them:

The "Z" has a hooked end stroke: This person is very egotistical and greedy. The more you give this person, the more he takes you for granted.

The "u" has a hook on the second stroke: suggesting someone who is vindictive and mean. The person will remember for ten years how you crossed him negatively.

The "t" looks like a tent with a flying cross: This person is probably disloyal and mean. Do you really want a person like that in your life?

The "t" looks like the number "7": This is the mark of a ruthless person. Her approach to solving problems is to use an axe rather than a scalpel. This writer has a lot of hurt feelings.

The "t" is laid way back and thick: You really want to avoid this type. The person might be bad tempered, aggressive and cruel.

The "o" looks like an onion: This person is probably a liar and a cheater. If you did not see his handwriting you would never even suspect that he would lie to you.

The "t" is slanted and thick: indicating a very bad temper. He will let you have it with all his might.   BEWARE!!

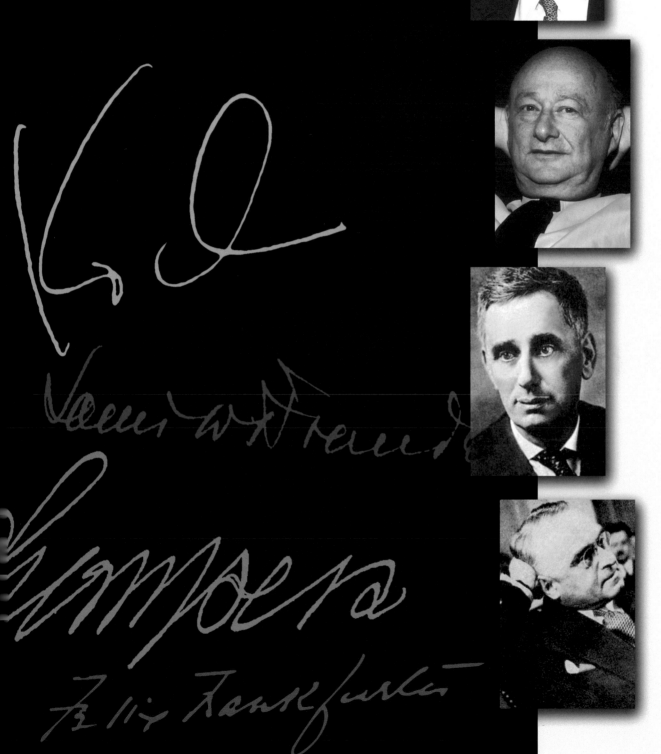

politicians

henry KISSINGER

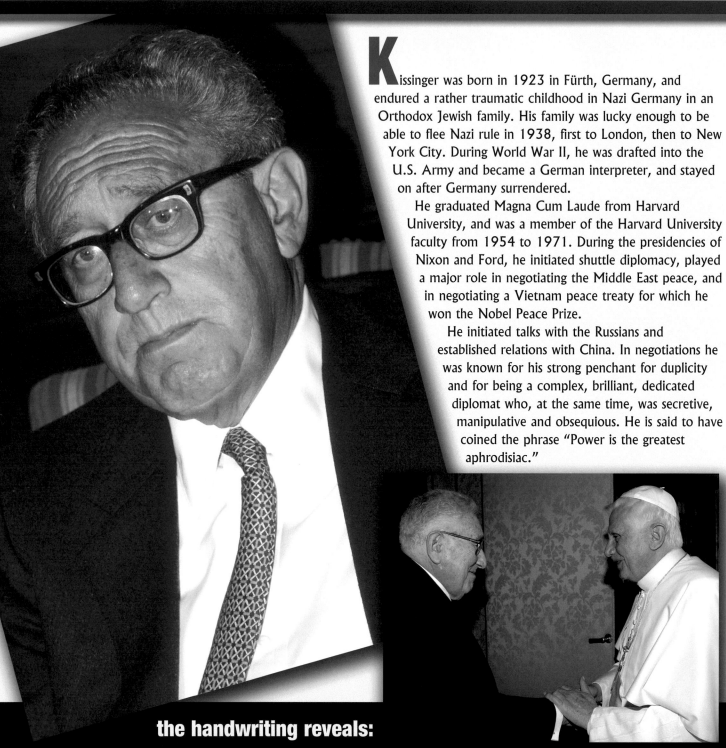

Kissinger was born in 1923 in Fürth, Germany, and endured a rather traumatic childhood in Nazi Germany in an Orthodox Jewish family. His family was lucky enough to be able to flee Nazi rule in 1938, first to London, then to New York City. During World War II, he was drafted into the U.S. Army and became a German interpreter, and stayed on after Germany surrendered.

He graduated Magna Cum Laude from Harvard University, and was a member of the Harvard University faculty from 1954 to 1971. During the presidencies of Nixon and Ford, he initiated shuttle diplomacy, played a major role in negotiating the Middle East peace, and in negotiating a Vietnam peace treaty for which he won the Nobel Peace Prize.

He initiated talks with the Russians and established relations with China. In negotiations he was known for his strong penchant for duplicity and for being a complex, brilliant, dedicated diplomat who, at the same time, was secretive, manipulative and obsequious. He is said to have coined the phrase "Power is the greatest aphrodisiac."

the handwriting reveals:

- A very high IQ
- Displays vigilant tendencies with powerful motives to make things happen.
- A clever and shrewd personality.
- A huge ego, with a strong need for approval.

He is said to have coined the phrase, "Power is the greatest aphrodisiac."

1. The large space between the **"t"** and the **"o"** indicates a person who always calculates before reacting.

2. The dash dot on the **"i"** suggests an irritable personality, possibly veiled by a sense of external calm.

3. The elongated **"d"** shows a cool, emotionally restrained person.

4. The swirling loop on the cross bar of the **"t"** indicates the writer is very egotistical and concerned about his image.

5. The flat hump in the **"h"** is typical for a person who is more diplomatic than confrontational.

6. The sharp descending **"f"** suggests a subconscious filled with hostility. The writer has a penetrating mind but also must always be in control.

7. The thread-like signature shows a personality that is diplomatic, evasive, non-confrontational.

"The Big Apple" has a lot to thank Ed Koch for: First and foremost, he restored it to fiscal stability after it went bankrupt during the1970s.

1. The **"p"** is pumped up, suggesting unresolved issues with sexuality.

2. The **"o"** is open, showing a tendency to speak one's mind.

3. The **"a"** has a double circle to the right, indicating extreme evasiveness.

4. The **"d"** has an overly-inflated stem, meaning open-minded, with overly emotional tendencies.

5. The **"t"** is wavy, suggesting a fighter and a stubborn personality accompanied by high sensitivity to criticism.

6. The **"y"** loop has a hooked end stroke, associated with altruism and a subconscious issue that continues to be repressed, which can cause problems.

7. A very full **"g"** loop, meaning strong materialistic and sexual tendencies.

160

ed KOCH

The City of New York has a lot for which to thank Ed Koch. First and foremost, he restored the city to fiscal stability after it went bankrupt during the 1970s. He was also responsible for placing the City on a GAAP (Generally Accepted Accounting Practices) balanced budget basis, with 10 such balanced budgets during his administration.

Koch began his career during World War II as a draftee into the Army. He came back a decorated soldier in 1946, and entered NYU's prestigious School of Law. He began practicing right after graduation, but could not resist the pull of politics. In 1968 was elected to the US House of Representatives, where he served for nine years. In 1977 he was elected mayor of New York City, and was re-elected for three consecutive terms.

Koch has returned to private practice, writes commentaries for television and radio, and is a columnist. Most recently he took over as judge on the "People's Court" television program.

the handwriting reveals:

- The writer can be very direct and to the point.
- A very colorful personality, with a vivid imagination. He is constantly checking other peoples' motives and intentions.
- Has confidence in his accomplishments.
- He can be very opinionated and on a subconscious level does not seem to forget past offenses.

louis BRANDEIS

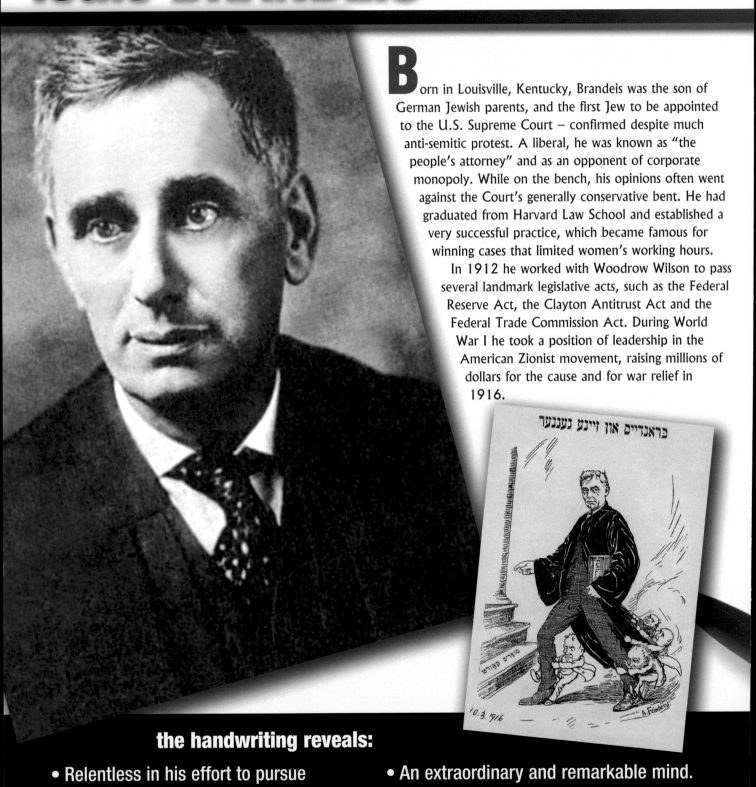

Born in Louisville, Kentucky, Brandeis was the son of German Jewish parents, and the first Jew to be appointed to the U.S. Supreme Court – confirmed despite much anti-semitic protest. A liberal, he was known as "the people's attorney" and as an opponent of corporate monopoly. While on the bench, his opinions often went against the Court's generally conservative bent. He had graduated from Harvard Law School and established a very successful practice, which became famous for winning cases that limited women's working hours.

In 1912 he worked with Woodrow Wilson to pass several landmark legislative acts, such as the Federal Reserve Act, the Clayton Antitrust Act and the Federal Trade Commission Act. During World War I he took a position of leadership in the American Zionist movement, raising millions of dollars for the cause and for war relief in 1916.

the handwriting reveals:

- Relentless in his effort to pursue whatever goals he set out to achieve.

- Very high need for clarity and meticulousness in his thinking process.

- An extraordinary and remarkable mind.

- Very highly developed sense of humor. He could be cute, funny and caring. On the other hand, he could have spells of rage and anger.

He was known as "the people's attorney" and as an opponent of corporate monopoly.

1. The down-stroke of the **"9"** is club-like, suggesting a great deal of aggression and a pursuit of one's goals with power and relentlessness.

2. A hooked lower zone – A great deal of altruism and sublimation of natural drives.

3. The **"i"** dot is dashed, indicating a powerful and impatient mind.

4. The **"d"** is looped at the stem, meaning a strong sense of self protectiveness.

5. The **"C"** is over-hooked, indicating an ability to memorize detail and pride in oneself.

6. The **"a"** is double-looped, revealing some kind of self-deception.

Under his leadership, the AFL grew from 150,000 to over 3 million members. His aim: to keep the union free from political entanglements.

1. The **"S"** looks locked at the bottom, showing a need to be secretive at times.

2. The **"S"** is hooked at the top, suggesting he did not let go of troubling ideas.

3. The **"m"** looks like a saw, suggesting a very analytical mind, and someone who could lose his temper at times.

4. The **"p"** is looped, showing a great sense of curiosity.

5. The **"r"** is pointed – again, a tremendously perceptive and probing mind.

AMERICAN FEDERATION OF LABOR

LFL. A. F. OF L BUILDING

Executive Council.
President, SAMUEL GOMPERS.
Secretary, FRANK MORRISON.
Treasurer, DANIEL J. TOBIN,
233 E. Michigan St., Indianapolis, Ind.

LONG DISTANCE TELEPHONE MAIN 3871-2-3-4-5-6
CABLE ADDRESS, AFEL

Washington, D.C. October 14, 1921.

Prof. V. Y. Russell,
1109 Hasbrook Street
Kansas City,

My dear Sir:-

    Enclosed you will please find list of pamphlets published by this office. If you can make use of any of these in your work as teacher of history, I shall be glad to send them to you but, of course, this does not include the A. F. of L. History Encyclopedia and Ready Reference Book, the AMERICAN FEDERATIONIST, or the printed proceedings of annual conventions of the A. F. of L.

    Hoping to hear from you further, I am,

                    Very truly yours,

                    President,
        American Federation of Labor.

samuel GOMPERS

Samuel Gompers, one of the earliest and most powerful leaders of the labor movement in the United States, was born in London. His family emigrated to America during the Civil War, and he, at the age of 14, joined the cigar makers' union.

Ten years later, he became its president, and helped to found what became the American Federation of Labor. During his leadership, the organization grew from 150,000 to over 3 million members. He guided the AFL through the Homestead and Pullman strikes, World War I and other tests of its solidarity. His aim: to keep the union free from political entanglements, socialistic ideas, and radical programs, maintaining that more wages, shorter hours, and greater freedom were the just aims of labor.

the handwriting reveals:

- Highly charismatic, colorful and vigorous; could win people over.

- Forceful and energetic, a go-getter approach to problem solving.

- Controversial with an ability to manipulate events to his favor.

- Detests authority figures and doesn't take "no" for an answer.

felix FRANKFURTER

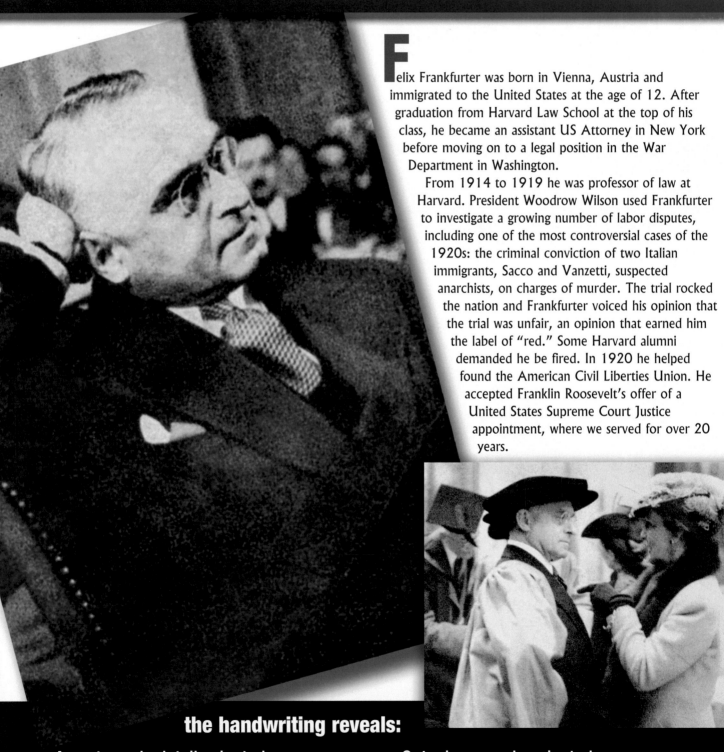

Felix Frankfurter was born in Vienna, Austria and immigrated to the United States at the age of 12. After graduation from Harvard Law School at the top of his class, he became an assistant US Attorney in New York before moving on to a legal position in the War Department in Washington.

From 1914 to 1919 he was professor of law at Harvard. President Woodrow Wilson used Frankfurter to investigate a growing number of labor disputes, including one of the most controversial cases of the 1920s: the criminal conviction of two Italian immigrants, Sacco and Vanzetti, suspected anarchists, on charges of murder. The trial rocked the nation and Frankfurter voiced his opinion that the trial was unfair, an opinion that earned him the label of "red." Some Harvard alumni demanded he be fired. In 1920 he helped found the American Civil Liberties Union. He accepted Franklin Roosevelt's offer of a United States Supreme Court Justice appointment, where we served for over 20 years.

the handwriting reveals:

- An extremely detail-oriented personality.

- A relentless fighter for perfection and high standards.

- Outgoing, people-oriented.

- High-strung energy with impatience towards slow processes; he hurried toward the future.

Frankfurter voiced his opinion that the Sacco and Vanzetti trial was unfair – an opinion that helped earn him the label of "red."

1. The **"R"** is a tight loop, showing a great deal of obstinacy and temper.

2. The **"g"** stem is looped and contained, suggesting some sexual disappointments.

3. The **"t"** cross bar is pretty far right of the stem, indicating a future-oriented personality, energetic and relentless in pursuing goals.

4. The **"e"** is like a Greek letter, denoting a highly cultured person.

5. The **"w"** is very high, expressing intellectual arrogance.

Jews & War

Jews are one of the most persecuted peoples in the history of the world. As the traditional Passover passage says, "in every generation there are enemies raised to destroy the Jews." The best answer for modern Israel, especially after the Holocaust resulted in the slaughtering of more than six million Jews, was to build up a legendary army. Israel knows that they don't have the luxury that practically every other nation has: namely, to lose a war and survive.

War of Independence (1948): Hours after Israel became a nation again, and David Ben-Gurion read the Declaration of Independence at the Tel Aviv Museum, each surrounding Arab country started to attack. They outnumbered the Jews by the millions, yet Israel built up an army with extreme passion, dedicated to making sure they wouldn't be wiped out. The number of casualties was the highest ever in Israeli history, and even though they were sufficiently outnumbered Israel conquered her attackers, and established borders of the Jewish state that would last until 1967.

The Sinai Campaign (1956): Nasser, the president of Egypt locked the Suez Canal, amassed troops along Israel's borders and blocked Israel's shipping routes to Africa and the rest of the Middle East. The French, British and Israelis tried to break the siege. Israel ended up withdrawing from the Sinai and Gaza, and enjoyed about 10 years of relative peace; the Egyptians refused to open the Suez Canal to Israeli shipping.

Six day War (1967): Egypt, Syria, Jordan and Iraq converged to destroy Israel in 1967. The Israeli Air Force took just five hours to demolish enemy airfields and gained absolute superiority in the air. This war's greatest prize was the liberation of Jerusalem. Since 1967, the Wailing Wall and the site of the Temple have been back in Jewish hands.

Yom Kippur War (1973): This war was by far the most humbling experience in the life of the Jewish state. In spite of intelligence warnings, Israel was unprepared for massive invasions from both Syria and Egypt on one of the holiest days in the Jewish calendar. The number of casualties was so high that a public uproar resulted in Prime Minister Golda Meir's resignation. However, from the Jewish point of view, a miracle occurred: The Syrian army was about to cut Israel in two, but they decided to wait a day. That one day allowed the Jews to reorganize and win the war.

Operation Peace for Galilee (1982)
In this conflict, Israel decided to go after Palestine Liberation Organization members harbored in southern Lebanon; they had been conducting terrorist activities and shelling Israeli settlements in the North. The Israeli Defense Forces (IDF) succeeded in routing the PLO in Lebanon, which moved its headquarters to Tunis. The operation inside Lebanon lasted for three years, much longer than expected, to the tune of 650 Israeli soldiers dead.

"You armed me with strength for battle;
you made my adversaries bow at my feet.
You made my enemies turn their backs in flight,
and I destroyed my foes."

2 Samuel 22:40-41

israelis

simon WIESENTHAL

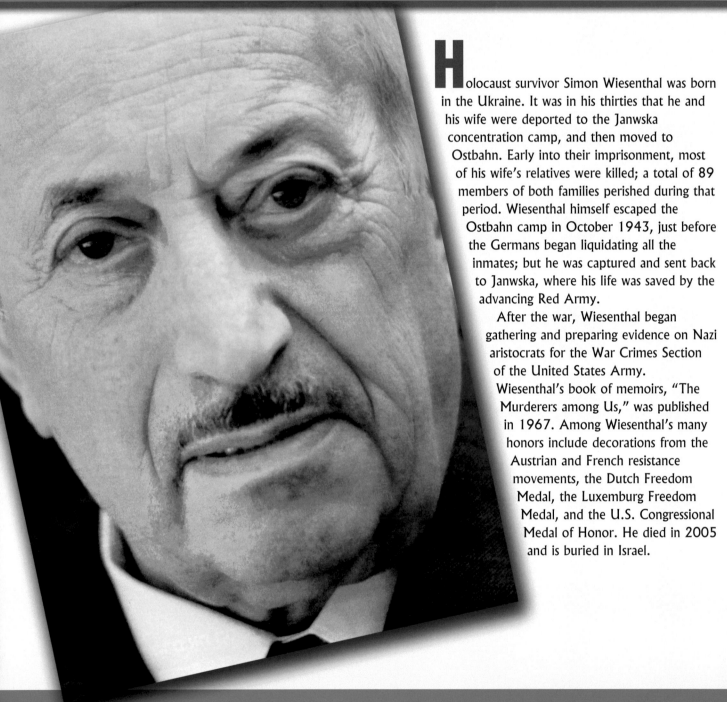

Holocaust survivor Simon Wiesenthal was born in the Ukraine. It was in his thirties that he and his wife were deported to the Janwska concentration camp, and then moved to Ostbahn. Early into their imprisonment, most of his wife's relatives were killed; a total of 89 members of both families perished during that period. Wiesenthal himself escaped the Ostbahn camp in October 1943, just before the Germans began liquidating all the inmates; but he was captured and sent back to Janwska, where his life was saved by the advancing Red Army.

After the war, Wiesenthal began gathering and preparing evidence on Nazi aristocrats for the War Crimes Section of the United States Army.

Wiesenthal's book of memoirs, "The Murderers among Us," was published in 1967. Among Wiesenthal's many honors include decorations from the Austrian and French resistance movements, the Dutch Freedom Medal, the Luxemburg Freedom Medal, and the U.S. Congressional Medal of Honor. He died in 2005 and is buried in Israel.

the handwriting reveals:

- Complex personality; lived as if he were still under siege.

- A personality in siege; subconsciously feeling as if behind barbed wire.

- Strong, demanding personality, very hard to please.

- Tendency to be self-absorbed.

A total of 89 members of both his and his wife's families perished.

1. His signature reflects major psychological turmoil. The interwoven loops and the ambiguousness of the signature are indicators that he has major reservations against exposing his true self to the public eye.

2. The signature also looks like barbed wire – which is reminiscent of his past as a prisoner in a concentration camp. Subconsciously he seemed to view the world as a place from which he had to protect himself.

Wiesenthal, the Jewish Nazi hunter.

The Jewish hero and general who crossed the bridge during the 1973 Yom Kippur war and saved Israel from destruction.

1. The text says, "I am a farmer; I don't need to be a politician." Note how the letter **"Nun"** looks like a plow in the soil. It shows a need to deal with powerful requirements and impulses in his life.

2. The letter **"Tav"** has an arm. It indicates a giving person.

3. The letter **"Lamed"** is one of the spiritual letters in Hebrew. It ends in the upper zone. Here you can see the spiritual qualities of the writer. His subconscious desires are often fighting with his conscious ones.

4. The letter **"Gimel"** looks like a pregnant woman, and indicates a subconscious need to not let go of what he has.

5. The final **"Tzadik"** indicates a person who likes confrontation, and likes to do the opposite of what others want him to do.

ariel SHARON

Ariel (Arik) Sharon was a kibbutz baby. After finishing agricultural school, he joined the Hagana, an underground Jewish resistance group formed in response to the British mandate on Palestine. He made a name for himself as a commander of an elite commando unit in Jordan and Egypt in the 1950s.

A brigadier general during the Yom Kippur war, he was the first to lead soldiers across the Suez Canal, and turned Israel's destiny around into one of favorable accomplishments. During the 1982 war in Lebanon, he was blamed for the massacre of Muslim Lebanese refugees by Christian Lebanese forces allied with Israel. Later, he oversaw the settlement of the West Bank as Menachem Begin's infrastructure minister. In 2000, he won a landslide election against Ehud Barak as a prime minister.

Sharon has two children, but unfortunately lost his first and second wives to cancer. He still has a farm in the Negev.

the handwriting reveals:

- A complicated, non-conformist personality.

- Ready for combat.

- Driven, with lots of tenacity.

- May be difficult to get along with.

the "i"

The **"i"** and its dot are another important combination of strokes for the graphologist. The dot can be written in various ways, reflecting the personality of the writer in a way that other letters can't. It enables us to glimpse the writer's true nature in the areas of:

Dexterity: The ideally dexterous person places the dot right above an "i" that is straight up and down.

Concentration: Again, the dot in the "right" place means the writer has exerted effort and concentration and is not distracted. Careful placement of the dot can also indicate that the person is either too pedantic, nit-picky, hypercritically fussy or dishonest. On the positive side, he can be detail-oriented, a realist and steady.

Stamina: In a long sample of writing the "i" tells us a lot about how long someone can keep with a detailed job. You don't want to hire a secretary that, after half a page, loses concentration.

This week I will be going to Milwaukee

The copy book dot: the baseline of measurement. This shows a person that adheres to reasonable social standards and needs to be clear in his communication to the people around him.

Saturday Afternoon, ill be going to Robinsons.

The round dot: indicates a careful and deliberate personality. This person might spend too many psychological resources doing the right thing to be "ok," at the expense of true self expression.

i

The low dot: shows a practical and objective personality. It may also mean low aspirations, fear of venturing out and a dread of changes. This person clings to the known and seeks to maintain status quo. He can be very vigilant and serious when it comes to short-term goals.

On Thursday morning I will be going to Chicago to attend the Convention

The moderately high dot: reveals someone with moderate aspirations, but who is still seeking some improvement and advancement in life. But his or her ambitions aren't overblown – they're practical.

i

The very high dot: This person lacks realism. The person is not able to base his life and performance on practical ideas. But he or she has a very good imagination, possibly with very high standards.

Think about a baby that crawls away from its mother. The more secure the baby is, the farther away she can wander. In social encounters, the space between you and the other person you talk to is a direct outcome of your personality. There are people who put their face into yours and there are those who seem to stand two miles away.

i

The heavy dot: The writer is decisive, firm, assertive and has a great deal of vitality. This person is also obsessed with detail. He can be very nasty and demanding of himself and others. He expects those around him to perform to his high level of standards.

On Saturday morning I will be going to Milwaukee to the Palette Shop.

The jabbed dot: It is more difficult to draw a dot then to dash it. If a person doesn't have patience, the dash is jabbed. This writer may often display a nasty temper and irritability.

On Friday afternoon I am flying to New York City.

The downwardly jabbed dot: shows anger and criticism directed towards oneself. The parents of this writer were probably tough and criticizing on the child's behavior and conduct.

í ì

The dashed dot: a powerful type, full of energy and assertive; the writer has a good sense of reality. On the other hand, he or she can be aggressive with a bad temper – and possibly even violent.

I will be going to

The crescent right dot: The writer is vivacious and full of humor, a good observer and fully determined. The will power of the writer is high and persistent. She can also be fun-loving.

On Wednesday afternoon, I will

The crescent left dot: emotionally reflective and full of dreams. On the negative side, this person tends toward neurosis and is distrustful. He or she most likely shuns the system.

i

The circle dot: This is a person who is attention seeking and who thrives on recognition. It might also indicate an artistic inclination or someone who actually practices art.

golda MEIR

Golda Meir was born in Kiev, Ukraine, in 1898. Victims of persecution, she and her family settled in Milwaukee in 1906. At the age of 11, she organized her first community project to raise money for the poor children who could not afford schoolbooks. She began giving speeches and became a gifted orator.

In a dispute with her parents, she ran away to Denver while a teenager; there, she met David Ben Gurion and Yitzhak Ben Tzvi, whom the Turks had banished from Palestine. They were recruiting volunteers who would help free Israel from Turkish rule. She talked her husband into moving to a kibbutz in late 1917. In 1936 she rose to the head of the political department of what later became the ruling party. In 1948 she raised $50 million from American Jews for the newly-founded state of Israel. In early 1969 she was named the Prime Minister, the first female prime minister of the world. She retired from political life soon after the Yom Kippur War of 1973 and died in 1978.

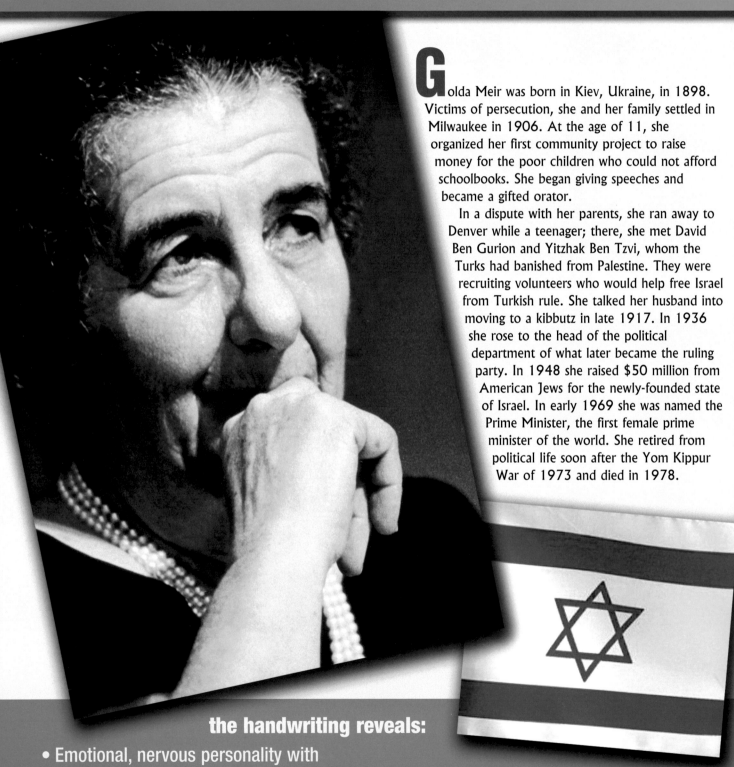

the handwriting reveals:

- Emotional, nervous personality with disdain for slow thinkers.

- Strong sense of being a protective mother to those underneath her.

- A bulldozer type, a single minded personality who tackled problems head-on.

- Great attention to detail.

At the age of 11, she organized her first community project to raise money for the poor children who could not afford schoolbooks – and became a gifted orator.

1. A looped starting stroke, indicates muddled thoughts.

2. The "o" is knotted on the left indicating deceptive tendencies.

3. An arched beginning stroke: a desire to take on responsibility.

4. The "i" dot is very high, meaning a nice imagination and a visionary.

5. However, the "i" dot is jabbed downward, meaning a tendency to criticize oneself.

6. The "r" is pointed, indicating a very aggressive mind.

He led the struggle to establish the State of Israel in May 1948.

1. The **"D"** has a long, tall first stroke and then curly: extremely entrepreneurial personality who also could exercise caution at times.

2. The dot over the **"i"** is roof-shaped indicating a very sharp thinker who liked to solve mysteries.

3. The **"y"** lower loop penetrates to the line below: his emotional needs overcame his ego.

4. The **"t"** cross bar covers two letters signifying a very assertive and go-getter personality.

5. The end stroke is like a knife, indicating a willingness to attack people who stand in the way of one's accomplishments.

15 Sdeh. Boker, 10. 11. 63
Dear Mr H. K. Thompson ⑤
In reply to your letter I must ③ ④
confess that I never read Rockwell
Kent's works, and to my regret
I am unable to make any contri
bution ② as you desire
Yours sincerely
①
D. Ben-Gurion

david BEN-GURION

David Ben-Gurion was born in Plonsk, Poland in 1886 to an ardent Zionist family; by his mid-teens, he was already a Zionist activist. Arriving in Palestine in 1906, he helped found the first Kibbutz, as well as the Jewish self-defense group, "Hashomer" (The Watchmen). He traveled on behalf of the Socialist-Zionist causes to New York, where he met and married Paula Monbesz, a fellow Poalei Zion activist.

He founded the Israeli trade unions and led the struggle to establish the State of Israel in May of 1948. He became Prime Minister and Defense Minister. In late 1953, Ben-Gurion left the government, but took the prime minister position back some years later. He supported the establishment of relations with West Germany, despite bitter opposition. In June 1963 Ben-Gurion resigned as Prime Minister for the last time, citing "personal reasons," and in 1970 retired from political life and returned to his home Kibbutz, where he passed away in 1973.

the handwriting reveals:

- Very realistic personality; down to earth, got things accomplished.

- Extremely strong personality: could run the opponent into the ground.

- Natural leadership qualities, sense of pride, with enough power to withstand political challenges.

- Once he set his mind to conquer a problem, he applied courage, self-esteem and listened to his intuition without worrying what others thought.

moshe DAYAN

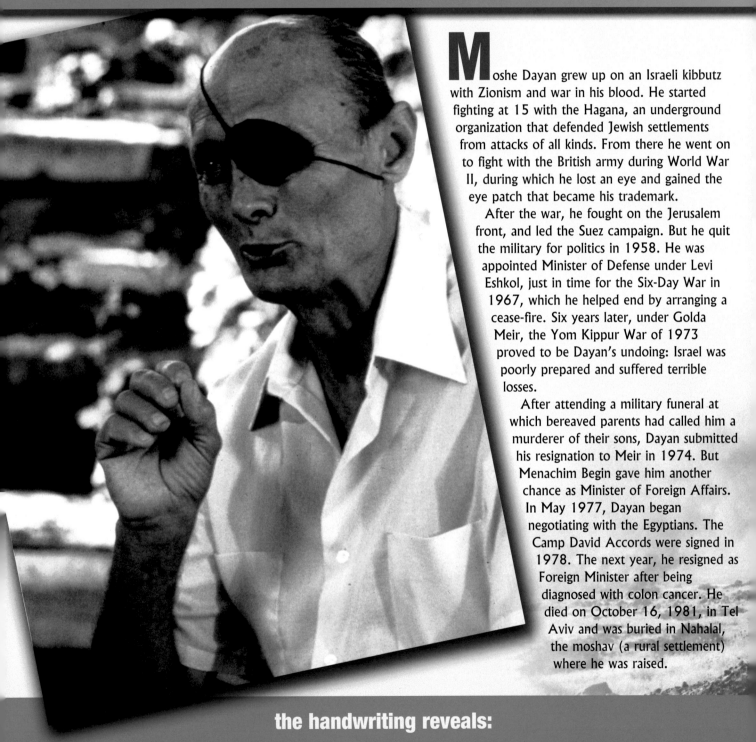

Moshe Dayan grew up on an Israeli kibbutz with Zionism and war in his blood. He started fighting at 15 with the Hagana, an underground organization that defended Jewish settlements from attacks of all kinds. From there he went on to fight with the British army during World War II, during which he lost an eye and gained the eye patch that became his trademark.

After the war, he fought on the Jerusalem front, and led the Suez campaign. But he quit the military for politics in 1958. He was appointed Minister of Defense under Levi Eshkol, just in time for the Six-Day War in 1967, which he helped end by arranging a cease-fire. Six years later, under Golda Meir, the Yom Kippur War of 1973 proved to be Dayan's undoing: Israel was poorly prepared and suffered terrible losses.

After attending a military funeral at which bereaved parents had called him a murderer of their sons, Dayan submitted his resignation to Meir in 1974. But Menachim Begin gave him another chance as Minister of Foreign Affairs. In May 1977, Dayan began negotiating with the Egyptians. The Camp David Accords were signed in 1978. The next year, he resigned as Foreign Minister after being diagnosed with colon cancer. He died on October 16, 1981, in Tel Aviv and was buried in Nahalal, the moshav (a rural settlement) where he was raised.

the handwriting reveals:

- A unique, non-conformist personality.

- Astutely quick thinker.

- Able to see his own faults and improve, with a strong need to express himself as clearly as possible

- Much more complex than meets the eye.

He grew up on an Israeli kibbutz with Zionism and war in his blood.

1. The **"M"** end stroke is like an arrow, indicating a go getter in interpersonal relations and career-oriented activities. Capable of stepping on other people's toes to achieve objectives.

2. In the **"M"** all humps are even, good executive ability.

3. The **"D"** shows two separate strokes, implying a strong sense of individualism and occasional difficulties in adjusting to reality.

4. The end stroke extended to the left implying he had a sense of his own importance.

5. The **"a"** is open at the top and leans to the right signifying a certain amount of emotional sincerity. Also indicates a talkative nature.

6. The **"y"** loop is exceedingly full, indicating strong hedonistic needs that could interfere with performance.

7. Final **"n"** is long and looks like a thread: associated with evasiveness. Hard to pin down such personalities.

The brilliant linguist, orator and debater Abba Eban helped spearhead post-war Israeli history; but his glorious career ended in defeat.

1. The **"l"** is like a baby curled up. Could be related to unresolved father issues.

2. The **"y"** loop is like a hook indicating a lack of physical fulfillment.

3. The **"t"** cross bar above the stem denotes a visionary personality.

4. The writing slant varies between left and right: ambivalence regarding being close or remaining distant with people. Might indicate that he had a critical father who was too strict.

5. The **"i"** dot is very high and slanted to the right implying a very fast thinker who used creativity and fantasy.

6. The **"E"** like the Greek letter: he was a very learned and cultured person.

November 17. 1973

I send you my warm personal greetings and my appreciation of your attendance at the American Technion Society's Dinner in honor of my friend Samuel Neaman — a great servant of noble causes

Abba Eban

abba Eban

Abba Eban was born Aubrey Solomon and educated at Queens College in Cambridge, England. He was a brilliant linguist and an outstanding orator and debater. In 1942 Eban served the Jewish community in Jerusalem as Allied Headquarters' Liaison Officer for the training of volunteers. In 1944 he became Chief Instructor at the Middle East Arab Center in Jerusalem.

He, in effect, became the chief spokesperson for the fledgling state and with his oratory genius, was able to articulate the Jewish state's case with great effectiveness at the United Nations, on American television, and before audiences around the world. He served as Israel's ambassador to the United States, yet yearned to return to Israel and become a political leader there. He spent the years from 1958 to 1966 as president of the Weizmann Institute in Rehovot. He was minister for foreign affairs from 1966 to 1974, serving during both the 1967 Six-Day War and the 1973 Yom Kippur War. Together with Golda Meir and Defense Minister Moshe Dayan, Eban was forced to resign from the government in March 1974 because of overwhelming public criticism for permitting Israel to be caught so unprepared on the eve of the Yom Kippur War.

He wrote a number of well-received books and memoirs, notably "Voice of Israel" (1957), "My People" (1968), "My Country" (1972), and "Diplomacy for a Next Century," (1998).

the handwriting reveals:

- One of the true geniuses presented in this book; his mind operated on levels that are incomprehensible to many people.

- Tendency to misjudge emotionally his effect on other people.

- His sheer intellectual superiority may have caused a tendency to display a short temper and to be easily frustrated.

- Although the writer was very sharp, he tended to hide his unique abilities.

Modern Israel & the Bible's Influence

Many people ask whether there is any connection between Jews today and the Jews as they lived during the days of Abraham the patriarch. The answer is yes!

Jews have been living, working, worshipping and thriving in the "Holy Land" since the time of Abraham. Through the most devastating wars and mass migrations of Jews out of their homeland and into other lands, there were always families that found ways to remain in Galilee.

Israel is a religious state, a Jewish State, which was made official in the Declaration of Independence by Ben-Gurion. That, by itself, established the continuity of Israel from the days of Abraham to present day; a legitimate rationale to counter some Arab sentiments regarding the Jews as foreign invaders. Later the Knesset passed "The Law of Return," which grants all Jews the right to immigrate and receive Israeli citizenship. No other country has this kind of immigration provision.

Thirdly, observance of festivals in Israel links the modern nation to the ancient one. Passover is a good example. The entire Jewish nation today observes Passover just as it had thousands of years ago. Plus, there is Bible study, which has been the thread linking the generations together. Whether they had to pray and study in private during times of persecution or able to study freely in their villages and cities, the Torah commands the Jewish people to "read it day and night;" so, studying the Torah is mandatory in Israeli schools six days a week from age eight to eighteen.

Yet another tie to the past is the observance of the Sabbath. In Israel, public transportation halts and shops are closed on Saturday. A famous Jewish saying maintains that "It is not so much that the Jews 'keep the Sabbath,' but more like the 'Sabbath keeps the Jews'." However, not all Israelis are fervently religious; Israel is split between an extremely observant and zealous population that maintain a conservative interpretation of the Torah, and one that is more liberal and believes in a need to adjust the Bible and its commandments to the modern era.

Another similarity between today's Israel and the nation of long ago is the fact that because of its unique connection to God, and positioning in the world, its neighbors, just as in the old days, are constantly threatening the country. Israel remains in a perpetual state of anticipated siege. As the Scripture implies, in every generation there are those who want to annihilate the Jews and wipe them from the face of the earth. So, they have inherited a unique tradition; one of survival by their wits. They have to outsmart the enemy.

And there still exists the common thread of Israel's spiritual foundation, the faith in one God, and the Covenant that God made with Abraham about the Promised Land. That First Commandment and God's promises stand as a beacon; the core spiritual belief hanging over the national identity of modern Israel. The Israelis feel they live in their spiritual homeland which they weren't able to do for generations. They are not guests. They have a national identity that cannot be destroyed.

Furthermore, the ancient Kosher dietary laws persist in Israel. In school cafeterias, army barracks, universities, hotels and other institutions, all food served is Kosher, meaning no pork or shell-fish, no mixing of meat and dairy, and so on. It adds to the cohesiveness of the culture, and bolsters Israeli Jews in their self-image as The Chosen People. Plus, don't forget the ongoing practice of circumcision, which in Hebrew is called "Brit," literally, a pact with God. Ironically, one of many customs the Jews and Arabs share.

*"See, I have given you this land.
Go in and take possession of the land
that the Lord swore
he would give to your fathers —
to Abraham, Isaac and Jacob —
and to their descendants after them."*

Deuteronomy 1:8

ilan RAMON

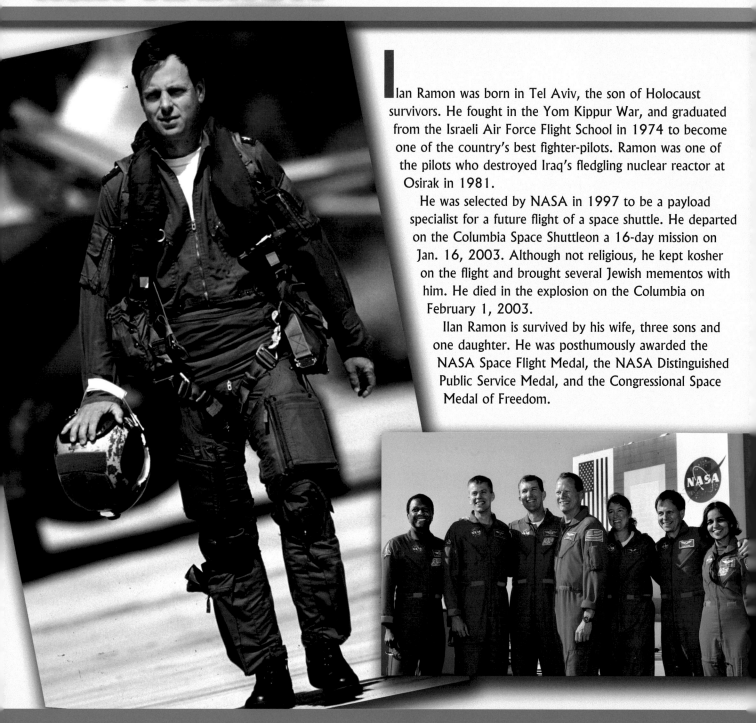

Ilan Ramon was born in Tel Aviv, the son of Holocaust survivors. He fought in the Yom Kippur War, and graduated from the Israeli Air Force Flight School in 1974 to become one of the country's best fighter-pilots. Ramon was one of the pilots who destroyed Iraq's fledgling nuclear reactor at Osirak in 1981.

He was selected by NASA in 1997 to be a payload specialist for a future flight of a space shuttle. He departed on the Columbia Space Shuttleon a 16-day mission on Jan. 16, 2003. Although not religious, he kept kosher on the flight and brought several Jewish mementos with him. He died in the explosion on the Columbia on February 1, 2003.

Ilan Ramon is survived by his wife, three sons and one daughter. He was posthumously awarded the NASA Space Flight Medal, the NASA Distinguished Public Service Medal, and the Congressional Space Medal of Freedom.

the handwriting reveals:

- Highly spiritual personality.

- Unpretentious, and in touch with himself.

- A strong ego, good problem solver.

- Methodical thinker with an insatiable curiosity for new discoveries.

> "I carry on the suffering of the Holocaust generation, and I'm kind of proof that despite all the horror they went through, we're going forward." – Ilan Ramon

1. The upper zone of his handwriting is well-developed. Working in the upper zone signifies a person who was spiritual and idealistic.

2. The curving **"l"** indicates a diplomatic personality who knew to keep his mouth shut when needed. It also shows deep analytical thinking.

3. The middle zone is very harmonious, which demonstrates a straightforward, go-getter personality.

4. The way the **"n"** (final letter in "Ilan") descends and interrupts the **"L"** in the line below hints at a personality in constant struggle between idealism and realism.

5. When Hebrew handwriting slants right, it indicates a warm, optimistic, friendly and creative person.

6. The way he smoothly and crisply went from his upper zone to his lower zone shows a deep thinker who was adept at problem-solving.

conclusion

This book is an exploration into the personalities of some of the most famous Jewish celebrities. Through that exploration, it shines light on the enormous contribution Jews have made to the world. Through graphology we discover many facets of these celebrities' true personalities and the enigmatic catalysts behind what actually makes them tick. The celebrities represented here represent just the tip of the iceberg.

The Jewish people, who make up less than half of a percent of the world's population, have had a significant effect on the world's cultural, scientific, artistic, economic, and literary development. While an overwhelming number of ancient peoples have disappeared from the face of the earth, the Jews seem to have somehow managed to stick around. Through heartfelt devotion to their culture, homeland, people and God, they have endured centuries of hardship, exile, persecution, slavery, and the list goes on.

Jews have always lived in the land that is now the nation of Israel, once called Canaan. Canaan was the land promised to Abraham and the Patriarchs of the Jewish people, according to the Old Testament of the bible. The Exodus story brought them back as a nation of "God's chosen people" to the Promised Land of Canaan where Joshua lead the Israelites across the Jordan River to the land promised to their forefathers. There have always been Jews in the land of Israel.

Jewish achievers have also been great trendsetters: Geniuses like Einstein, Oppenheimer, Bohr, Fermi and Isador Rabi were all Nobel Prize winners. David Ben-Gurion, Gold Meir, and Moshe Dayan put the Jewish State back on the map. Athletes Mark Spitz and Sandy Koufax broke multiple world records. Sigmund Freud introduced humanity to psychology/psychiatry. Bernard Baruch and Helena Rubinstein made remarkable advances within their respective industries. Neil Simon and Arthur Miller pioneered their own genres that forever changed the way plays would be written and performed. Henry Kissinger opened China to the West. Leonard Bernstein and at least a dozen other composers helped define American musical culture.

Within the roots of Judaic culture lies the belief that the world was created in six days and that on the seventh day, God rested. For the Jews, this demonstrates that the world is still a work in progress, and one of their main duties is to finish the job and make the world a better place. It would appear that Jewish achievers have done and continue to do just that. As for being the Chosen People of God, it is a mixed blessing: Jews have paid dearly for the privilege, yet it aids them in never losing sight of hope.

photo credits

169   Beit Ariela Archives, Reuters
171   Monitin Magazine, October 1983
172   Shooting Star
173   David Silverman / Reuters, 1998
176   Shooting Star, Kessler Photography
177   Beit Ariela Archives
178   Kessler Photography
179   Shooting Star
180   Shooting Star
181   Ho New, Reuters, Kessler Photography
184   Beit Ariela Archives
185   Shooting Star
186   Reuters   Reuters
188   Beit Ariela Archives
189   Beit Ariela Archives

In this book Dr Robert Yaronne uncovers the psyches of some of the world's most famous Jews, based on their handwriting. There is much to learn from a graphological analysis of some of the greatest Jews in entertainment, politics, science, sports, finance, literature, philosophy, and spiritual leadership. Dr. Yaronne shines new light on celebrity lives from Hollywood to Israel, and beyond, by telling what handwriting reveals about intellect, subconscious motives, loves, fears, and drives. In addition, the book contains brief biographies and pertinent background information about Jews in history as well as principles of handwriting analysis.

Further Readings:

Jacobson, Simon. "Biography" in Menachem M Schneerson, Toward a Meaningful Life Morrow, NY, 1995

Lutke, Harvey. History in their Hands. A Book of Jewish Autographs. Jason Aronson, Northvale, N.J. 1996

Peterson, Pat. Fast Facts, Two Volumes. Self published. http://www.handwriting.org/main/hwabooks.html

Slater, Elinor and Robert. Great Jewish Women. Jonathan David Publishers, NY, 1994

Slater, Elinor and Robert. Great Jewish Men, 2d edition. Jonathan David Publishers, NY, 1998